The Ultimate POWER PRESSURE COOKER XL Cookbook

Over 100 Deliciously Easy Recipes for Busy Families, All 6 Ingredients or Less

by

Elizabeth Bradshaw

The Ultimate Power Pressure Cooker XL Cookbook:
Over 100 Deliciously Easy Recipes for Busy Families,
All 6 Ingredients or Less

Copyright © 2017 Elizabeth Bradshaw

ISBN: 978-1-945056-27-7

Book Design:
Velin@Perseus-Design.com

Cover photo credit: bhofack2/ Depositphotos.com

All photos from Depositphotos.com

Back cover: All photos from Depositp hotos.com
gbh007, ryzhkov86, barakudka, belchonock

All interior photos - Depositphotos. com
com udra p. 3, Telesh p. 6 & 7, tycoon p. 13,
Mizina p. 17, bhofack2 p. 20, Mizina p. 25, gresey
p. 26, barakudka p. 29, ennar p. 31, livertoon
p. 32, asimojet p. 35, robynmac p. 36, barakudka
p. 40, HandmadePicture p. 43, bergamont p. 45,
HandmadePicture p. 49, lenyvavsha p. 52, Southern
Light Studios p. 55, photographee. eu p. 59,
lenyvavsha p. 60, rafalstachura p. 63, lenyvavsha
p. 64, rafalstachura p. 71, lenyvavsha p. 73,
alisafarov p. 74, asimojet p. 77, stu99 p. 80,
bhofack2 p. 83, piccaya p. 84, Blinztree p. 87,
lenyvavsha p. 88, photominer p. 91, ezumeimages
p. 92, vdeineka.yandex.ru p. 99, Hannamariah
p. 100, Odelinde p. 103, bhofack2 p. 104, Shebeko p.
107, manyakotic p. 109, asimojet p. 110, lenyvavsha
p. 115, a41cats p. 116, manyakotic p. 118,
Anjela30 p. 122, lenyvavsha p. 125, belchonock
p. 126, BreamChub p. 129, livfriis p. 130, alisafarov
p. 137, asimojet p. 138, manyakotic p. 141,
resnick_joshua1 p. 142, bhofack2 p. 147, sarsmis
p. 148, ryzhkov86 p. 151, komarmaria p. 154,
photominer p. 157, lenyvavsha p. 158, aremafoto
p. 163, bhofack2 p. 164, ryzhkov86 p. 167,
lenyvavsha p. 168, bhofack2 p. 172, neillangan
p. 175, photominer p. 176, joannawnuk p. 181,
belchonock p. 183, raptorcaptor p. 185, ingridhs
p. 186, Sasajo p. 189, HHLtDave5 p. 190,
belchonock p. 193

Legal Disclaimer
The information contained in this book is the
opinion of the author and is based on the author's
personal experience and observations. The author
does not assume liability whatsoever for the use of
or inability to use any or all information contained
in this book, and accepts no responsibility for any
loss or damages of any kind that may be incurred
by the reader as a result of actions arising from the
use of information in this book. Use this information
at your own risk. The author reserves the right
to make any changes he or she deems necessary
to future versions of the publication to ensure its
accuracy.

Welcome to The Ultimate Power Pressure Cooker XL Cookbook! Maybe you are a first time Power Pressure Cooker XL user, looking for simple meals to sharpen your skills. Or perhaps you've already figured out that the Power Pressure Cooker XL is the way to go to prepare meals fast, but need some fresh ideas for simple, easy meals. Either way, this book is packed with step by step instructions that are easy to follow and meal ideas that are lacking in long lists of ingredients, but not lacking in flavor!

Just a little about this book….***The Ultimate Power Pressure Cooker XL*** Cookbook was written to be a guide to prepare fast, easy meals with things we typically have on hand or can find easily at the local grocer using 6 ingredients or less. I think it's nice to be armed with a great selection of easy recipes for busy, hectic days. A savvy chef could easily use these recipes as a starting point and add even more wonderful flavor to the dish. However, all of these recipes are delicious just as they are written.

When I say Six Ingredients, I mean six ingredients, plus a few others that I assume everyone with a kitchen will have on hand. These include things like salt, pepper, cooking oil and water. Other than that, all the recipes in this book contain six ingredients, or less. A few of the recipes offer optional ingredients for extra flavor or garnish. I think this book proves that simple can be delicious!

You will find that some of these recipes contain canned or jarred ingredients. I try to be health conscious, but there are days when my schedule just doesn't permit me to make all of my own sauces and seasoning mixes. For those days, I am grateful to be able to pull out a jar of something and still give my family a home cooked meal. Of course, in any of these recipes, feel free to substitute a homemade version of any sauce or spice mix.

The Power Pressure Cooker XL has certainly revolutionized today's cooking with its ability to prepare dishes quickly and make the food delicious and savory. Yet in today's busy life, there are some days that we still need the simplest version. I hope this book will inspire you to create some excellent meals for yourself and your loved ones.

BENEFITS OF COOKING WITH THE POWER PRESSURE COOKER XL

The Power Pressure Cooker XL is quickly changing the way meals are prepared in kitchens all around the world. Gone are the days of unsafe pressure cookers and stories of food exploding all over the kitchen. The Pressure Cooker XL has undergone rigorous testing and is foolproof and safe. Simply put, the machine will not build pressure unless the lid is securely fastened and locked. And the lid is designed so that it cannot be removed while the machine is under pressure. This means you can create delicious, restaurant quality meals in your home without the fear of any unsafe or unsavory messes.

This machine is designed to be user friendly and features a stainless steel exterior and a non-stick inner pot for easy cleaning. There is a digital control panel with pre-programmed cook times to take the guesswork out of most meals. In addition to being used as a pressure cooker, this appliance also has the capability to be a canner, slow cooker, steamer and perfect rice cooker.

Understanding the Power Pressure Cooker XL, is as easy as understanding the functions on the digital display panel. All of the pre-programmed buttons, with the exception of the Canning/Preserving and Slow Cook functions, cook at the same pressure and temperature. You only have to select the button that is closest to your desired pressure cooking time. This book makes that step extremely simple, by already selecting the appropriate buttons to use for each recipe.

POWER PRESSURE COOKER FUNCTION KEYS

Keep Warm/Cancel Button

This is used to stop the cooking process when the pressure cooker is programmed and still in effect. When the timer goes of on your pressure cooker, it will automatically switch into Keep Warm/Cancel mode while pressure begins to release. This function can be used to keep food warm before serving.

Time Adjustment Button

Use this button to increase the minutes a recipe is cooked. For example, for a recipe calling for 12 minutes of pressure cooking time, you would select the Soup/Stew button (10 minutes) and then use the Time Adjustment button to reach a 12 minute cook time.

Chicken/ Meat Button

This function is usually the best option for meat and chicken with pre-programmed cook times of 15, 40 and 60 minutes. This setting is also the best option for browning or searing meats or vegetables before cooking under pressure.

Fish/ Vegetable/Steam Button

The best option for seafood or for steaming and is pre-programmed for 2,4 and 10 minutes.

Beans/ Lentils

The Beans/ Lentils feature is pre-set for times of 5, 15 and 30 minutes making it a great option for cooking most dried beans and lentils, as well as other recipes.

Rice/Risotto

This button is pre-programmed for 6, 18 and 25 minutes. Typically it is 6 minutes for white rice, 18 minutes for brown rice and 25 minutes for wild rice.

Slow Cook

This feature makes your Power Pressure Cooker XL extremely versatile by turning it into a slow cooker with temperature range from174-199 degrees Fahrenheit and cook time from 2-12 hours.

Soup/Stew

The Soup/Stew button is the best option of creating a perfect pot of soup or a tender stew. The pre-programmed times are 10, 30 and 60 minutes.

Canning/ Preserving

This button turns your pressure cooker into a pressure canner, all at the touch of a button. This selection cooks at a higher pressure and temperature than all of the other pre-set buttons. It is pre-programmed for 10,45 and 120 minutes.

Delay Timer

This feature allows you to program the appliance to start cooking at a later time in the day.

Cook Time Selector

This function allows you to select one of the pre-programmed times on any of the other buttons. It is a quick way to adjust to a greater amount of time. For example, if a recipe calls for 40 minutes under pressure using the Meat/ Chicken button, you would simply select the Meat/Chicken button and then hit the Cook Time Selector button once to select the pre-programmed time of 40 minutes.

Program Buttons	Default Time	Quick-Medium-Well Select Button
Delay Timer	N/A	N/A
Canning/Preserving	10 minutes	10/45/120 minutes
Soup/Stew	10 minutes	10/30/60 minutes
Slow Cook	2 hours	2/6/12 hours
Rice/Risotto	6 minutes	6/18/25 minutes
Beans/Lentils	5 minutes	5/15/30 minutes
Fish/Veg/Steam	2 minutes	2/4/10 minutes
Meat/Chicken	15 minutes	15/40/60 minutes

PRESSURE COOKING TIME TABLES

MEAT (POULTRY, BEEF, PORK AND LAMB)

Meat Types	Cooking Time (in Minutes)
Beef, stew meat	15 to 20
Beef, meat ball	10 to 15
Beef, dressed	20 to 25
Beef, pot roast, steak, rump, round, chuck, blade or brisket, large	35 to 40
Beef, pot roast, steak, rump, round, chuck, blade or brisket, small chunks	25 to 30
Beef, ribs	25 to 30
Beef, shanks	25 to 30
Beef, oxtail	40 to 50
Chicken, breasts	8 to 10
Chicken, whole	20 to 25
Chicken, cut up with bones	10 to 15
Chicken, dark meat	10 to 15
Cornish Hen, whole	10 to 15
Duck, cut up with bones	10 to 12
Duck, whole	25 to 30
Pheasant	20 to 25
Turkey, breast, boneless	15 to 20
Turkey, breast, whole, with bones	25 to 30
Turkey, drumsticks (leg)	15 to 20
Quail, whole	8 to 10
Lamb, cubes	10 to15
Lamb, stew meat	10 to 15
Lamb, leg	35 to 45
Ham slice	9 to 12
Ham picnic shoulder	25 to 30
Pork, loin roast	55 to 60
Pork, butt roast	45 to 50

Meat Types	Cooking Time (in Minutes)
Pork, ribs	20 to 25
Veal, chops	5 to 8
Veal, roast	35 to 45

SEAFOOD AND FISH

Fish and Seafood Types	Cooking Time in Minutes (Fresh)	Cooking Time in Minutes (Frozen)
Crab	3 to 4	5 to 6
Fish, whole	5 to 6	7 to 10
Fish fillet	2 to 3	3 to 4
Fish steak	3 to 4	4 to 6
Lobster	3 to 4	4 to 6
Mussels	2 to 3	4 to 5
Seafood soup or stock	6 to 7	7 to 9
Shrimp or Prawn	1 to 2	2 to 3

RICE AND GRAINS

Rice & Grain Varieties	Water Quantity (Grain : Water ratios)	Cooking Time (in Minutes)
Barley, pearl	1:4	25 to 30
Barley, pot	1:3 ~ 1:4	25 to 30
Congee, thick	1:4 ~ 1:5	15 to 20
Congee, thin	1:6 ~ 1:7	15 to 20
Couscous	1:2	5 to 8
Corn, dried, half	1:3	25 to 30
Kamut, whole	1:3	10 to 12
Millet	1:1 2/3	10 to 12
Oats, quick cooking	1:1	6
Oats, steel cut	1:1 2/3	10
Porridge, thin	1:6 ~ 1:7	15 to 20
Quinoa, quick cooking	1:2	8
Rice, Basmati	1: 1.5	4 to 8
Rice, Brown	1: 1.25	22 to 28
Rice, Jasmine	1: 1	4 to 10

Rice & Grain Varieties	Water Quantity (Grain : Water ratios)	Cooking Time (in Minutes)
Rice, white	1: 1.5	8
Rice, wild	1:3	25 to 30
Sorghum	1:3	20 to 25
Spelt berries	1:3	15 to 20
Wheat berries	1:3	25 to 30

FRESH OR FROZEN VEGETABLE

Vegetable Types	Cooking Time in Minutes (Fresh)	Cooking Time in Minutes (Frozen)
Artichoke, whole, trimmed without leaves	9 to 11	11 to 13
Artichoke, hearts	4 to 5	5 to 6
Asparagus, whole or cut	1 to 2	2 to 3
Beans, green/yellow or wax, whole, trim ends and strings	1 to 2	2 to 3
Beets, small roots, whole	11 to 13	13 to 15
Beets, large roots, whole	20 to 25	25 to 30
Broccoli, flowerets	2 to 3	3 to 4
Broccoli, stalks	3 to 4	4 to 5
Brussel sprouts, whole	3 to 4	4 to 5
Cabbage, red, purple or green, shredded	2 to 3	3 to 4
Cabbage, red, purple or green, wedges	3 to 4	4 to 5
Carrots, sliced or shredded	1 to 2	2 to 3
Carrots, whole or chunked	2 to 3	3 to 4
Cauliflower flowerets	2 to 3	3 to 4
Celery, chunks	2 to 3	3 to 4
Collard	4 to 5	5 to 6
Corn, kernels	1 to 2	2 to 3
Corn, on the cob	3 to 4	4 to 5
Eggplant, slices or chunks	2 to 3	3 to 4
Endive	1 to 2	2 to 3
Escarole, chopped	1 to 2	2 to 3
Green beans, whole	2 to 3	3 to 4

Vegetable Types	Cooking Time in Minutes (Fresh)	Cooking Time in Minutes (Frozen)
Greens(beet greens, collards, kale, spinach, swiss chard, turnip greens), chopped	3 to 6	4 to 7
Leeks	2 to 4	3 to 5
Mixed vegetables	2 to 3	3 to 4
Okra	2 to 3	3 to 4
Onions, sliced	2 to 3	3 to 4
Parsnips, sliced	1 to 2	2 to 3
Parsnips, chunks	2 to 4	4 to 6
Peas, in the pod	1 to 2	2 to 3
Peas, green	1 to 2	2 to 3
Potatoes, in cubes	7 to 9	9 to 11
Potatoes, whole, baby	10 to 12	12 to 14
Potatoes, whole, large	12 to 15	15 to 19
Pumpkin, small slices or chunks	4 to 5	6 to 7
Pumpkin, large slices or chunks	8 to 10	10 to 14
Rutabaga, slices	3 to 5	4 to 6
Rutabaga, chunks	4 to 6	6 to 8
Spinach	1 to 2	3 to 4
Squash, acorn, slices or chunks	6 to 7	8 to 9
Squash, butternut, slices or chunks	8 to 10	10 to 12
Sweet potato, in cubes	7 to 9	9 to 11
Sweet potato, whole, small	10 to 12	12 to 14
Sweet potato, whole, large	12 to 15	15 to 19
Sweet pepper, slices or chunks	1 to 3	2 to 4
Tomatoes, in quarters	2 to 3	4 to 5

DRIED BEANS, LEGUME AND LENTILS

Dried Beans & Legume Types	Cooking Time in Minutes (Dry)	Cooking Time in Minutes (Soaked)
Adzuki	20 to 25	10 to 15
Anasazi	20 to 25	10 to 15
Black beans	20 to 25	10 to 15
Black eyed peas	20 to 25	10 to 15
Chickpeas (chick peas, garbanzo bean or kabuli)	35 to 40	20 to 25

Dried Beans & Legume Types	Cooking Time in Minutes (Dry)	Cooking Time in Minutes (Soaked)
Cannellini beans	35 to 40	20 to 25
Gandules (pigeon peas)	20 to 25	15 to 20
Great Northern beans	25 to 30	20 to 25
Lentils, French green	15 to 20	N/A
Lentils, green, mini (brown)	15 to 20	N/A
Lentils, red, split	15 to 18	N/A
Lentils, yellow, split (moong dal)	15 to 18	N/A
Lima beans	20 to 25	10 to 15
Kidney beans, red	25 to 30	20 to 25
Kidney beans, white	35 to 40	20 to 25
Navy beans	25 to 30	20 to 25
Pinto beans	25 to 30	20 to 25
Peas	15 to 20	10 to 15
Scarlet runner	20 to 25	10 to 15
Soy beans	25 to 30	20 to 25

FRUITS

Fruit Types	Cooking Time in Minutes (Fresh)	Cooking Time in Minutes (Dried)
Apples, in slices or pieces	2 to 3	3 to 4
Apples, whole	3 to 4	4 to 6
Apricots, whole or halves	2 to 3	3 to 4
Peaches	2 to 3	4 to 5
Pears, whole	3 to 4	4 to 6
Pears, slices or halves	2 to 3	4 to 5
Prunes	2 to 3	4 to 5
Raisins	N/A	4 to 5

TABLE OF CONTENTS

DIPS AND SAUCES 17

BUFFALO CHICKEN DIP 18

HOT CRAB DIP 19

ARTICHOKE AND SPINACH DIP 21

HOMEMADE MARINARA SAUCE 22

HOT SAUCE 23

APPLE SAUCE 24

SOUPS, STEWS AND CHILIS .. 25

CREAMY SAUSAGE ORZO SOUP 26

PORK AND CABBAGE SOUP 29

CHICKEN TACO SOUP 30

CHILI 33

CHICKEN VEGETABLE SOUP 34

TOMATO RICE CHICKEN SOUP 35

CREAMY PUMPKIN SOUP 37

SIDE DISHES, PASTAS AND RICE 39

ROASTED VEGETABLES 40

CORN ON THE COB 41

HONEY-SOY SAUCE GLAZED MIXED MUSH-ROOMS 42

BRAISED BABY BOK CHOY WITH PROSCIUTTO 43

SOUTHERN STYLE GREEN BEANS WITH BACON 44

SWEET AND ORANGEY BRUSSELS SPROUTS .. 46

POTATO SALAD 47

BAKED BEANS 48

BASIC RISOTTO 50

COCONUT PANDAN RICE 51

CINNAMON ORANGE RICE PILAF 52

RAGU ELBOW PASTA WITH VEGETABLES 55

GNOCCHI IN CHEESY ALFREDO SAUCE 56

SEAFOOD 57

SHRIMP TIKKA MASALA 59

CRAB CAKES WITH ROASTED PEPPER SAUCE . 60

CAJUN SHRIMP AND ASPARGUS 61

MAHI MAHI IN GREEN CHILE SAUCE 62

WHITE FISH IN TAMARIND BROTH 63

HERBED GARLIC SALMON FILLET 64

BEEF 67

MEATBALLS IN TOMATO-BASIL SAUCE 69

BEEF STROGANOFF 70

BEEF BBQ 72

BEEF CURRY 73

CHIPOTLE BEEF BARBECUE BRISKET 74

ITALIAN SHREDDED BEEF 76

EASY POT ROAST 79

BBQ SHORT RIBS 80

MEATLOAF 83

BEEF STRIPS IN AU JUS GRAVY 84

SLOPPY JOES 87

CRANBERRY BEEF BRISKET 88

BEEF AND BROCCOLI 89

CHILI BARBECUE STEAKS 90

BEEF IN CREAMY MUSHROOM SAUCE 91

SWEET AND SAVORY MEATBALLS 94

SPAGHETTI WITH CHUNKY TOMATO MEAT SAUCE 95

SAUCY SHREDDED BEEF 97

CORNED BEEF 99

CHIPOTLE BEEF POT ROAST 100

CHICKEN 103

CHICKEN ADOBO 105

CHICKEN PROSCIUTTO ROLLS 106

STICKY GARLICKY CHICKEN 107

CHICKEN WITH WHITE CREAM SAUCE 108

CHICKEN IN BLACK BEAN SAUCE 111

CHICKEN IN CHEESY SUN-DRIED TOMATO
SAUCE 113

SPICY PEANUT CHICKEN TENDERS 114

CHICKEN CURRY 116

HAWAIIAN BBQ CHICKEN 117

HONEY MUSTARD CHICKEN 118

CHICKEN AND DUMPLINGS 121

ASIAN STYLE BARBECUE CHICKEN 122

WHOLE ROAST CHICKEN 125

CHICKEN ALFREDO 126

CHICKEN IN LEMON GARLIC SAUCE 127

CHEESY STUFFED CHICKEN IN
ALFREDO SAUCE 128

CHICKEN MARSALA 129

HONEY GLAZED CHICKEN TENDERS 132

BRAISED CHICKEN IN MOLE SAUCE 133

APRICOT-ORANGE CHICKEN BREAST 134

MEXI-CALI CHICKEN 137

CAJUN CHICKEN 138

PINEAPPLE SALSA CHICKEN 139

ROSEMARY LEMON CHICKEN 140

ORANGE CRANBERRY TURKEY BREAST ... 143

PORK 145

PORK AFRITADA 146

APRICOT GLAZED PORK TENDERLOIN 147

PORK CHOPS WITH MUSHROOM GRAVY 148

PLUM SAUCED PORK RIBS 151

CHIPOTLE PORK LOIN 152

SAUSAGE AND PEPPERS 153

PORK IN SWEET BLACK BEAN SAUCE 154

KALUA PORK 156

GLAZED HONEY HAM 159

HICKORY SMOKED BARBECUE PORK RIBS 160

PORK CARNITAS 163

BRAISED HONEY-DIJON PORK BELLY 164

BARBECUE PULLED PORK 165

PORK SAUSAGE IN ONION GRAVY 166

PORK CHOPS WITH DIJON SAUCE 168

PORK CHOPS AND APPLESAUCE 171

MUSTARD BARBECUE SPARERIBS 172

HAWAIIAN PORK ROAST 173

SMOKY BARBECUE BABY BACK RIBS 174

PORK CHOPS WITH RANCH GRAVY 176

DESSERTS 177

TAPIOCA PUDDING 178

SPICED STEWED PEARS 181

STEWED MIXED FRUITS 182

CRANBERRY-APPLE SAUCE 185

MINI MOLTEN CHOCOLATE CAKES 186

THREE LAYER MAGIC CAKE 188

Dips and Sauces

BUFFALO CHICKEN DIP

An excellent and easy dip to serve at your next party. You can use the hot sauce recipe in this book or just the jarred variety from the store. Be sure to have lots of chips for serving. This dip will go fast!

Ingredients:

- 2 chicken breasts, pounded thin
- 1 package of cream cheese (8 ounces)
- 1 packet Ranch dip seasoning
- 1 cup hot sauce
- 2 cups shredded cheddar cheese
- 1 stick butter, melted

Preparation Time: 5 minutes
Cooking time: 25 minutes
Serves: 4-6

Directions:

1. Add together all ingredients in the inner pot of the pressure cooker, except for the cheddar cheese. Stir to combine.
2. Close the lid completely and slide the pressure valve to locked position.
3. Press the "Meat/ Chicken" button and cook for 15 minutes.
4. When the pressure cooking cycle is completed, slide the pressure valve to open position to fully release the pressure. Open the lid when pressure is released.
5. Shred the chicken and stir in the cheddar cheese until melted. Transfer into a serving bowl and serve with pita wedges or tortilla chips.

HOT CRAB DIP

When you are longing for the ocean, but are miles away, treat yourself to this delicious crab dip. Its simple to throw together and cooks up fast in your pressure cooker.

Ingredients:

- 1 (8 ounce) block cream cheese, softened
- ½ cup mayonnaise
- 1 cup chopped or shredded crab meat
- 1 tablespoon fresh lemon juice
- 1-2 teaspoon hot sauce
- 1 ½ cups shredded cheddar
- chopped scallions (optional)

Preparation time: 10 minutes
Cooking time: 20 minutes
Serves: 6 to 8

Directions:

1. Mix together all ingredients and season to taste. Pour into a heat-safe baking dish that fits in the inner pot of the pressure cooker.
2. Prepare a foil sling by folding an 18-inch aluminum foil twice. This is used to easily remove the baking dish from the pressure cooker after pressure cooking.
3. Pour 2 cups of water in the inner pot of the pressure cooker and add the steamer tray. Place the baking dish on the center of the foil sling and carefully place it on the tray
4. Close the lid completely and slide pressure valve to locked position.
5. Press the "Soup/ Stew" button which will cook the dip for 10 minutes.
6. When the pressure cooking cycle is completed, slide the pressure valve to open position to fully release the pressure. Open the lid when pressure has released.
7. Use the sling to pull the baking dish from the inner pot being careful as it will be hot. Serve immediately with pita wedges or tortilla chips.

ARTICHOKE AND SPINACH DIP

This is my mom's recipe for artichoke dip that I have adjusted to be made in the Power Pressure Cooker XL. Its an incredibly creamy and tasty dip thats sure to please the crowds at your next party.

Ingredients:

- 1 cup finely chopped frozen spinach
- 1 can finely chopped artichoke hearts, finely chopped
- 1 cup mayonnaise
- 1 cup shredded parmesan cheese
- 1 packet Italian dressing seasoning
- 1/3 sour cream
- Salt and black pepper, to taste

Preparation time: 10 minutes
Cooking time: 20 minutes
Serves: 6 to 8

Directions:

1. Mix together all ingredients and season to taste. Pour into a lightly greased heat-safe baking dish that fits in the inner pot of the pressure cooker.
2. Prepare a foil sling by folding an 18-inch aluminum foil twice. This is used to easily remove the baking dish from the pressure cooker after pressure cooking.
3. Pour 2 cups of water in the inner pot of the pressure cooker and add the steamer tray. Place the baking dish on the center of the foil sling and carefully place it on the steamer tray.
4. Close the lid completely and slide pressure valve to locked position.
5. Press the "Soup/ Stew" button which will set cooking time for 10 minutes.
6. When the pressure cooking cycle is completed, slide the pressure valve to open position to fully release the pressure. Open the lid when pressure has released.
7. Use the sling to pull the baking dish from the inner pot being careful as it will be hot. Serve immediately with pita wedges or tortilla chips.

HOMEMADE MARINARA SAUCE

Homemade marinara just tastes so much better than the jarred variety, and now making your own is quite simple. You can play with the mix of veggies and herbs to make the sauce to suit your own taste.

Ingredients:

- 3 cups of canned crushed tomatoes
- 2 teaspoons of minced garlic
- ½ cup minced shallots
- 1 cup diced carrot
- 2 tablespoons minced fresh basil
- 1 teaspoon mixed Italian herbs
- 1/4 cup water
- drizzle olive oil

Preparation time: 10 minutes
Cooking time: 45 minutes
Serves: 4 to 6

Directions:

1. In the inner pot of the pressure cooker, add a drizzle of olive oil and press the "Meat/Chicken" button. Add the garlic and shallots and sauté for about 2 to 3 minutes or until soft and tender. Stir in the rest of the ingredients and season to taste with salt and pepper. Press the "Keep Warm/Cancel" button and close the lid completely.
2. Slide pressure valve to locked position. Press the "Meat/ Chicken" button which will automatically set the pressure cooking time to 15 minutes.
3. When the pressure cooking cycle is completed, use the natural release method to fully release the pressure. Open the lid when pressure has released and float valve has dropped.
4. Adjust seasonings if desired, serve immediately or store in covered containers and place in the fridge or freezer for future use.

HOT SAUCE

Enjoy fresh hot sauce prepared in your kitchen. Make a batch of this to keep on hand for all of your cooking needs. Everyone will be so impressed that it is homemade!

Ingredients:

- 1 cup diced red chili peppers
- 1 cup apple cider vinegar
- 1 teaspoon minced garlic
- ½ teaspoon salt
- 1 teaspoon corn starch
- 2 tablespoons sugar

Preparation time: 5 minutes
Cooking time: 15 minutes
Serves: 8

Directions:

1. Combine together all ingredients in the inner pot of the pressure cooker and briefly stir to combine.
2. Close the lid completely and slide pressure valve to locked position.
3. Press the "Fish/Veg/Steam" button and the "Cook Time Selector" button to set the pressure cooking time to 4 minutes.
4. When the pressure cooking cycle is completed, slide the pressure valve to open position to fully release the pressure. Open the lid when pressure has released and let it rest to cool completely.
5. Transfer into a covered glass jar and chill before serving.

APPLE SAUCE

Power Pressure Cooker XL applesauce is one of the favorite things my family makes. In fact, my youngest will only eat homemade applesauce now! Use your favorite type of apple, or a variety of apples to make it as sweet or tangy as you desire.

Ingredients:

- 8-10 medium apples, peeled, cored and quartered
- 1 cup apple juice
- 2 to 3 teaspoons of ground cinnamon
- ½ teaspoon of ground nutmeg
- ½ teaspoon of ginger powder

Preparation time: 15 minutes
Cooking time: 45 minutes
Serves: 4 to 5

Directions:

1. Combine together the spices and apple juice in a bowl and set aside.
2. In the inner pot of the pressure cooker, place the apples and pour in the apple juice mixture. Make sure the apples don't go over the max capacity fill line on your Power Pressure Cooker XL.
3. Close the lid completely and slide pressure valve to locked position.
4. Press the "Rice/Risotto" button and use "Time Adjustment" button to set the pressure cooking time to 8 minutes.
5. When the pressure cooking cycle is completed, use the natural release method in fully releasing the pressure. Open the lid when pressure has released.
6. Place the apple mixture into a food processor and process until smooth. Let it rest to cool completely and transfer into sealed bottles or jars. Store it in the fridge for future use.

Soups, Stews and Chilis

CREAMY SAUSAGE ORZO SOUP

This is a soup I created with things I had on hand one night when it was too cold for me to want to venture out to the store. The result was an incredibly tasty soup that my family has prepared over and over again. The Italian sausage adds plenty of wonderful flavor, but feel free to add your favorite seasonings and spices to make it your own.

Ingredients:

- 1 pound sweet Italian sausage, casing removed
- 1 (15 ounce) can diced tomato
- 12 ounces orzo pasta
- 6 cups chicken broth
- 3/4 cup frozen spinach
- 1 cup heavy cream

Preparation time: 10 minutes
Cooking time: 35 minutes
Serves: 4 to 6

Directions:

1. Place the sausage in the inner pot of the pressure cooker and press the "Meat/Chicken" button. Cook until browned, then remove the sausage and drain the grease. Put the sausage back in the pot and add the tomato, chicken broth and spinach. Press the "Keep Warm/Cancel" button.
2. Close the lid completely and slide pressure valve to locked position.
3. Press the "Meat/Chicken" button which will automatically set the time for 15 minutes.
4. When the pressure cooking cycle is completed, slide the pressure valve to open position to fully release the pressure. Open the lid when pressure has released.
5. Add the orzo and cream to the pot. Close the lid and position pressure valve back to locked position. Press the "Fish/Veg/Steam" button and use "Time Adjuster" button to set time for 3 minutes.
6. When timer beeps, release the pressure manually. Open the lid when the float valve has dropped.
7. Taste and adjust the seasonings until the desired flavor is achieved and serve warm in individual serving bowls.

Creamy Sausage Orzo Soup | 28

PORK AND CABBAGE SOUP

This is such a simple and delicious soup that is packed with flavor. The pork will cook up perfectly in your pressure cooker and be nice and tender.

Ingredients:

- 1 1/2 pounds pork ribs, country style (boneless), cut into chunks
- 2 cups of chiffonade cut cabbage leaves
- 1 large carrot, peeled and diced
- 1 large russet potato, diced into bite-sized chunks
- 1 cup diced white onion
- 4 cups of canned chicken or vegetable broth bouillon
- salt and pepper or seasoning of choice

Preparation time: 15 minutes
Cooking time: 45 minutes
Serves: 6 to 8

Directions:

1. Season the cuts of pork evenly with salt and black pepper on both sides.
2. Place it in the inner pot of the pressure cooker and press the "Meat/Chicken" button. Cook until the sides are lightly browned while turning occasionally. Stir in the onion and carrots and cook until the vegetables are soft and tender.
3. Pour in the broth and potatoes and press the "Keep Warm/Cancel" button.
4. Close the lid completely and slide pressure valve to locked position.
5. Press the "Rice/Risotto" button and hit the "Cook Time Selector" button twice to set the pressure cooking time to 25 minutes.
6. When the pressure cooking cycle is completed, slide the pressure valve to open position to fully release the pressure. Open the lid when pressure has released.
7. Stir in the cabbage and adjust seasonings if needed. Press the "Meat/Chicken" button and cook until it returns to a boil. When cabbage has softened to desired level, press the "Keep Warm/Cancel" button.
8. Portion into individual serving bowls and serve it warm.

CHICKEN TACO SOUP

This soup has been a staple on my table since my mother began preparing it when I was in high school. Originally this recipe was designed for the slow cooker, but with just a few tweaks, this soup can be made in your Power Pressure Cooker XL and on the table in less than a half an hour. Serve with cornbread for a yummy treat.

Ingredients:

- 3-4 chicken breasts, diced
- 1 packet Ranch dressing seasoning
- 1 packet Taco seasoning
- 1 can diced tomatoes with chilies
- 2 cans black beans, drained and rinsed
- 1 can corn, with liquid
- 2 cups water

Preparation time: 5 minutes
Cooking time: 25 minutes
Serves: 6

Directions:

1. Add all the ingredients to the inner pot of your pressure cooker and stir.
2. Close the lid completely and slide pressure valve to locked position.
3. Press the "Soup/Stew" button which will set pressure cooking time to 10 minutes.
4. When the pressure cooking cycle is completed, slide the pressure valve to open position to fully release the pressure. Open the lid when pressure has released.
5. Adjust seasoning. Serve immediately with cheese, sour cream, or tortilla chips as toppings.

CHILI

This wonderful chili recipe is sure to warm and fill you up on a cold day. Use a mix of whatever beans you have on hand, such as kidney beans, black beans or pinto beans. Garnish with cheese, sour cream, cilantro or corn chips.

Ingredients:

- 1 ½ pounds of ground beef
- 1 small onion, diced
- 3 cans diced tomatoes with chilies
- 2 cans beans of your choice
- 2-3 tablespoons chili powder
- 1 tablespoon minced garlic
- 1 cup water
- drizzle oil
- Salt and pepper, to taste

Preparation time: 10 minutes
Cooking time: 30 minutes
Serves: 4 to 6

Directions:

1. In the inner pot of the pressure cooker, add the oil and press the "Meat/Chicken" button. Sauté the onion for about 2 to 3 minutes or until soft and tender. Add the garlic. Stir in the ground beef, season to taste with salt and pepper and cook until browned.
2. Stir in the remaining ingredients and mix well. Adjust seasonings to preferred level of spiciness. Press the "Keep Warm/Cancel" button.
3. Close the lid completely and slide pressure valve to locked position.
4. Press the "Soup/Stew" button which will set the pressure cooking time to 10 minutes.
5. When the pressure cooking cycle is completed, allow a natural release of the pressure for 15 minutes. Then slide the pressure valve to open position to fully release the pressure. Open the lid when pressure has released.
6. Adjust seasoning if desired, portion into individual serving bowls and serve immediately.

CHICKEN VEGETABLE SOUP

This is a simple soup with rustic, earthy flavors. Even picky eaters usually find this soup is enjoyable. Adjust the taste by adding your favorite seasonings and spices. Serve with a chunk of thick bread for dipping.

Ingredients:

- 1 pound cooked chicken breast, cut into cubes or shredded
- 1 15 oz. can of diced tomatoes
- 1 small white onion, diced
- 3 cups chicken broth
- 1 carrot, diced
- 2 cups of diced potatoes
- Salt, pepper or seasoning of choice, to taste
- drizzle olive oil

Preparation time: *15 minutes*
Cooking time: *15 minutes*
Serves: *8*

Directions:

1. In the inner pot of the pressure cooker, add the oil press the "Meat/Chicken" button. Add in the chicken, onion, carrot and potatoes and season to taste with salt and black pepper. Cook until the vegetables are lightly soft and tender and pour in the broth and diced tomatoes.
2. Press the "Keep Warm/Cancel" button.
3. Close the lid completely and slide pressure valve to locked position.
4. Press the "Meat/ Chicken" button which sets the pressure cooking time to 15 minutes.
5. When the pressure cooking cycle is completed, slide the pressure valve to open position to fully release the pressure. Open the lid when pressure has released.
6. Adjust seasoning if desired, portion into individual serving bowls and serve immediately.

TOMATO RICE CHICKEN SOUP

Ingredients:

- 2 tablespoons of butter
- 2 cups of canned, seasoned tomato sauce
- 1 cup of full cream
- 1 pound cooked chicken breast, cut into cubes or shredded
- 4 cups chicken broth
- 1/2 cup white rice, rinsed and drained
- Salt and pepper (or any preferred seasoning)

Preparation time: 5 minutes
Cooking time: 15 minutes
Serves: 4 to 6

Directions:

1. In the inner pot of the pressure cooker, add the butter and press the "Meat/Chicken" button. Add the chicken and tomato sauce and season to taste with salt and pepper. Cook for about 5 minutes while stirring occasionally. Pour in the stock and stir just to combine.
2. Press the "Keep Warm/Cancel" button.
3. Close the lid completely and slide pressure valve to locked position.
4. Press the "Meat/Chicken" button which sets the pressure cooking time to 15 minutes.
5. When the pressure cooking cycle is completed, slide the pressure valve to open position to fully release the pressure. Open the lid when pressure has released.
6. Stir in the cream, press the "Meat/Chicken" button and cook until it returns to a boil. Adjust seasoning if desired.
7. Portion into individual serving bowls and serve immediately.

CREAMY PUMPKIN SOUP

Ingredients:

- 1 15 oz. can of pumpkin puree
- ¼ cup of butter
- 3 cups of chicken broth
- 1 cup of heavy cream
- 1 cup of grated Parmesan cheese
- 1 teaspoon of Italian seasoning mix

Preparation time: 5 minutes
Cooking time: 10 minutes
Serves: 4 to 6

Directions:

1. In the inner pot of the pressure cooker, add all ingredients except the cheese and stir just to combine.
2. Close the lid completely and slide the pressure valve to locked position.
3. Press the "Soup/Stew" button and set the pressure cooking time to 10 minutes.
4. When the pressure cooking cycle is completed, slide the pressure valve to open position to fully release the pressure. Open the lid when pressure has released.
5. Stir in the cheese until it has melted. Portion into individual serving bowls and serve immediately.

Side Dishes, Pastas and Rice

This variety of healthy diced vegetables are a prefect and easy side dish to make in your Power Pressure Cooker XL.

ROASTED VEGETABLES

Ingredients:

- 1 cup diced sweet peppers
- 2 cups diced sweet potatoes
- 1 cup onion, diced
- 2 teaspoons of Italian seasoning mix
- ¼ cup of butter
- ¼ cup of water
- Salt and pepper, to taste

Preparation time: 10 minutes
Cooking time: 11 minutes
Serves: 6 to 8

Directions:

1. In the inner pot of the pressure cooker, add all ingredients and season to taste with salt and pepper. Stir to combine.
2. Close the lid completely and slide pressure valve to locked position.
3. Press the "Soup/Stew" button and use the "Time Adjustment" button to set time at 11 minutes.
4. When the pressure cooking cycle is completed, slide the pressure valve to open position to fully release the pressure. Open the lid when pressure has released.
5. Gently stir and adjust seasoning if desired. Transfer into a serving bowl and serve immediately.

CORN ON THE COB

The Power Pressure Cooker XL makes the best corn on the cob. Not only is it incredibly quick and easy, every time I have used it (which is often!) it makes the most perfectly cooked corn that is sweet and juicy. My family loves pressure cooked corn on the cob!

Ingredients:

- 4 fresh ears of corn, shucked
- Salt and ground black pepper, to taste
- Butter, for serving
- 2 cups of water

Preparation time: **5 minutes**
Cooking time: **15 minutes**
Serves: **4**

Directions:

1. In the inner pot of the pressure cooker, add 2 cups of water and place the steamer tray inside. Place the corn on the steamer tray and arrange it in a way to cook it evenly. You may need to cut the corn into halves to fit and arrange inside the pressure cooker.
2. Close the lid completely and slide pressure valve to locked position. Press the "Fish/Veg/Steam" button and set the pressure cooking time to 2 minutes.
3. When the pressure cooking cycle is completed, slide the pressure valve to open position to fully release the pressure. Open the lid when pressure has released. Remove the corn and transfer to a plate.
4. Lightly brush with butter, season to taste with salt and black pepper and serve immediately.

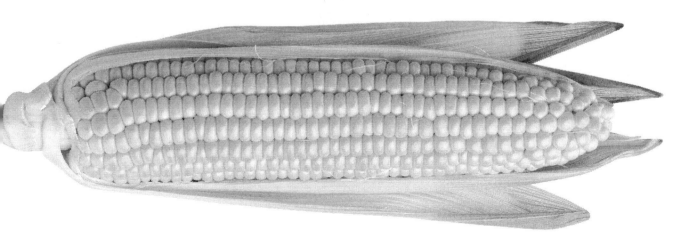

HONEY-SOY SAUCE GLAZED MIXED MUSHROOMS

These saucy mushrooms are the perfect accompaniment to your main dish, particularly steak of chicken.

Ingredients:

- 2 tablespoons of olive oil
- 2 teaspoons minced garlic
- 1 ½ pounds of mixed mushrooms
- ¼ cup vegetable or chicken stock
- ¼ cup honey
- 2 tablespoons of soy sauce

Preparation time: 5 minutes
Cooking time: 15 minutes
Serves: 4

Directions:

1. In the inner pot of the pressure cooker, add all ingredients and season to taste with salt and pepper. Stir to combine.
2. Close the lid completely and slide pressure valve to locked position.
3. Press the "Beans/Lentils" button which automatically sets the pressure cooking time to 5 minutes.
4. When the pressure cooking cycle is completed, slide the pressure valve to open position to fully release the pressure. Open the lid when pressure has released.
5. Gently stir and adjust seasoning if desired. Transfer into a serving bowl and serve immediately.

BRAISED BABY BOK CHOY WITH PROSCIUTTO

Bok choy has a flavor that, at least to me, is a combination of cabbage and brussel sprouts. Its delicious! If that sounds like something you would enjoy, this is a tasty recipe that is quite easy to prepare. It makes for an impressive presentation and the sauce is delicious.

Ingredients:

- 6 medium heads of baby bok choy, cut into half lengthwise
- 1 teaspoon garlic powder
- ½ cup vegetable or chicken stock
- ½ cup sliced prosciutto
- ¼ cup honey
- 2 tablespoons of soy sauce

Preparation time: 5 minutes
Cooking time: 15 minutes
Serves: 4

Directions:

1. In the inner pot of the pressure cooker, add all ingredients and stir to combine.
2. Close the lid completely and position the pressure valve to locked position.
3. Press the "Beans/Lentils" button which sets the pressure cooking time to 5 minutes.
4. When the pressure cooking cycle is completed, slide the pressure valve to open position to fully release the pressure. Open the lid when pressure has released.
5. Transfer to a serving platter and serve immediately.

SOUTHERN STYLE GREEN BEANS WITH BACON

We eat these green beans at least once a week and we never get tired of them. They are incredibly easy to make and get a healthy vegetable on the table in no time at all.

Ingredients:

- 1 ½ pounds of green beans, trimmed and snapped into halves
- 4-6 slices of thin bacon, diced
- ½ cup of diced white onion
- Salt and ground black pepper, to taste
- ½ teaspoon of garlic powder
- 1 cup of water or chicken stock

Preparation time: 10 minutes
Cooking time: 15 minutes
Serves: 4

Directions:

1. In the inner pot of the pressure cooker, press the "Meat/Chicken" button and add in the bacon. Cook for about 3 to 4 minutes, until beginning to brown. Add in the onions and cook until soft and translucent. Remove bacon, onion and bacon grease from inner pot and set aside.
2. Add 1 cup water or chicken stock to the pot and set in the steamer tray. Place green beans on top of the steamer tray. Season to taste with garlic powder, salt and pepper and press the "Keep Warm/Cancel" button.
3. Close the lid completely and slide pressure valve to locked position. Press the "Beans/Lentils" button which sets the pressure cooking time to 5 minutes.
4. When the pressure cooking cycle is complete, slide the pressure valve to open position to fully release the pressure. Open the lid when pressure has released.
5. Transfer the beans to a serving bowl. Pour in the bacon, onions and a bit of the bacon grease. Toss to combine and serve immediately.

SWEET AND ORANGEY BRUSSELS SPROUTS

I feel like brussel sprouts have become quite popular and for good reason! These delicious little cabbages are so flavorful and full of health benefits. Cooked in a sweetened orangey sauce, even those dubious about the brussel sprout will become a fan.

Ingredients:

- 1 ½ pounds of trimmed and halved Brussels sprouts
- 1 orange, zested and juiced
- 2 tablespoons of butter
- 1 ½ teaspoons Italian Seasoning (or dried herbs of choice)
- 2 tablespoons of raw honey or pure maple syrup
- ½ cup vegetable stock or water
- Salt and freshly ground black pepper, to taste

Preparation time: 5 minutes
Cooking time: 15 minutes
Serves: 4 to 6

Directions:

1. In the inner pot of the pressure cooker, add all ingredients and stir to evenly coat the Brussels sprouts with other ingredients. Season to taste with salt and pepper and close the lid completely. Position pressure valve to locked position. Press the "Fish/Veg/Steam" button and use "Time Adjustment" button to set the pressure cooking time to 3 minutes.
2. When the pressure cooking cycle is completed, slide the pressure valve to open position to fully release the pressure. Open the lid when pressure has released. Gently toss and adjust seasonings if desired.
3. Transfer to a serving bowl and serve immediately.

POTATO SALAD

Risotto cooked on the stovetop requires constant stirring and attention. But in the Power Pressure Cooker XL you can achieve perfectly cooked and delicious rice just by hitting a few buttons. This is a perfect side dish or add a side salad and have a complete meal.

Ingredients:

- 2 pounds medium sized russet potatoes, peeled and diced
- 3 eggs
- 1/4 cup onion or celery, your choice of crunch
- 1 cup mayonnaise
- 1/4 cup relish
- 1 tablespoon mustard
- salt and pepper, to taste
- 2 cups water
- fresh chopped dill for serving (optional)

Preparation time: **20** minutes
Cooking time: **20** minutes
Serves: **8**

Directions:

1. In the inner pot of the pressure cooker, add the water and place the steamer tray. Add the peeled and diced potatoes to the top of the steamer tray and place the eggs on top of the potatoes.
2. Close the lid completely and position pressure valve to locked position.
3. Press the "Fish/Veg/Steam" button and hit the "Cook Time Selector" button to adjust cooking time to 4 minutes.
4. When the pressure cooking cycle is completed, slide the pressure valve to open position to fully release the pressure. Open the lid when pressure has released. Pull out the eggs and submerge in an ice water bath to stop the cooking process. Pull potatoes out and set aside to cool.
5. In a large mixing or serving bowl, stir together the onion or celery, mayonnaise, relish and mustard. Gently fold in the potatoes when they are cooled, careful not to mix to harshly and mash them. Peel and dice the eggs and add to the potato salad. Season with salt and pepper and stir gently.
6. Place in the refrigerator and chill. Garnish with fresh chopped dill before serving if desired.

BAKED BEANS

Baked beans are a staple at any summer barbecue and are easy and delicious in the pressure cooker. You can play around with the flavors, adding more brown sugar if you like sweeter beans or more mustard if thats your preference.

Ingredients:

- 1 pound dried navy beans
- 6-8 slices bacon, diced into 1 inch pieces
- ½ cup ketchup or tomato sauce
- ¼ cup brown sugar
- 1-2 teaspoons mustard (depending on your taste)
- ½ cup molasses
- 10 ½ cups water, divided
- salt and pepper, to taste

Preparation time: 10 minutes
Cooking time: 1 hour, 25 minutes
Serves: 8

Directions:

1. Rinse and sort the beans, preparing them to soak. Add 8 cups of cool water to a pot, pour in the beans and allow to soak overnight.
2. Drain the beans and discard the water. Set beans aside.
3. Press the "Meat/Chicken" button and add the bacon to the inner pot of the pressure cooker. Cook until browned. Add ketchup, brown sugar, molasses, mustard and 2 ½ cups water to the pot. Stir in the beans and salt and pepper to taste. Press the "Keep Warm/Cancel" button.
4. Close the lid completely and position pressure valve to locked position. Press the "Meat/Chicken" button and hit the "Cook Time Selector" button two times to set the timer to 60 minutes.
5. When pressure cooking has completed the cooking cycle, allow pressure to release naturally for 15 minutes before performing a quick release.
6. Adjust seasonings if desired. If bean liquid is not desired consistency, press the "Meat/Chicken" button. Simmer beans, stirring frequently until sauce reaches desired thickness. Transfer to a serving bowl and serve immediately.

BASIC RISOTTO

Risotto cooked on the stovetop requires constant stirring and attention. But in the Power Pressure Cooker XL you can achieve perfectly cooked and delicious rice just by hitting a few buttons. This is a perfect side dish or add a side salad and have a complete meal.

Ingredients:

- 1 tablespoon of olive oil
- 1 cup diced onion
- 2 cups of starchy short grain rice (Arborio rice)
- 3 cups of vegetable or stock
- 1 tablespoon white wine
- 1 teaspoon of Italian seasoning mix, to taste

Preparation time: 5 minutes
Cooking time: 20 minutes
Serves: 4

Directions:

1. In the inner pot if the pressure cooker, add the oil and press the "Meat/Chicken" button. Sauté the onions until soft and add in the rice. Sauté for another 3 minutes and stir in the wine. Cook until the wine has reduced almost completely, add in the remaining ingredients and press the "Keep Warm/Cancel" button.
2. Close the lid completely and slide pressure valve to locked position.
3. Press the "Rice/Risotto" button and use "Time Adjustment" button to set the pressure cooking time to 8 minutes.
4. When the pressure cooking cycle is completed, slide the pressure valve to open position to fully release the pressure. Open the lid when pressure has released.
5. Fluff the rice with a spatula, transfer into a serving bowl and serve immediately.

COCONUT PANDAN RICE

If you are looking for a side dish with wonderful flavor and a bit of an ethnic feel, then look no further! Panda leaves are available at some local grocers, most Asian markets and also online. This recipe has amazing flavor and color.

Ingredients:

- 2 cups long-grain white rice
- 3 cups chicken stock
- ½ cup coconut milk
- 1 or 2 Pandan leaves, tied
- Salt and pepper, to taste
- 1 large pinch of salt

Preparation time: 5 minutes
Cooking time: 20 minutes
Serves: 4

Directions:

1. In the inner pot of the pressure cooker, add the all ingredients and season to taste with salt and pepper. Stir to combine.
2. Close the lid completely and slide pressure valve to locked position.
3. Press the "Rice/Risotto" button and use "Time Adjustment" button to set the pressure cooking time to 8 minutes.
4. When the pressure cooking cycle is completed, slide the pressure valve to open position to fully release the pressure. Open the lid when pressure has released. Discard Pandan leaves.
5. Fluff the rice with a spatula, transfer into a serving bowl or platter and serve immediately.

CINNAMON ORANGE RICE PILAF

The Power Pressure Cooker XL is well known for making tasty, perfectly cooked rice, so why not take your rice to the next level? This rice is infused with cinnamon and orange flavor and has a sprinkling of pistachios for a bit of added texture. The preparation will certainly add some excitement to everyday, plain rice!

Ingredients:

- 2 tablespoons clarified butter
- 2 cups of Jasmine rice, rinsed and drained
- 2 ½ cups of chicken stock
- ½ teaspoon of salt
- 1 teaspoon orange zest
- ½ teaspoon cinnamon
- 4 tablespoons pistachios

Preparation time: 5 minutes
Cooking time: 20 minutes
Serves: 4

Directions:

1. In the inner pot of the pressure cooker, combine together all ingredients and stir to combine.
2. Close the lid completely and position the pressure valve to locked position.
3. Press the "Rice/Risotto" button and use "Time Adjustment" button to set the pressure cooking time to 8 minutes.
4. When the pressure cooking cycle is completed, slide the pressure valve to open position to fully release the pressure. Open the lid when pressure has released.
5. Fluff the rice with a spatula, transfer into a serving bowl and top with more cinnamon and pistachios if desired. Serve immediately.

Cinnamon Orange Rice Pi...

RAGU ELBOW PASTA WITH VEGETABLES

The kids will love this one and its a great way to get them to eat their veggies. Most kids will happily gobble up pasta in a cheesy, tomato sauce, even if it is laced with a few vegetables. Use the pre-packaged frozen mixture or a variety of your favorite vegetables.

Ingredients:

- 2 cups jarred tomato sauce
- 2 cups precooked elbow pasta
- 1-2 cups frozen mixed vegetable of your choice
- 2 tablespoons white wine
- 1 teaspoon Italian seasoning mix
- ¼ cup grated Parmesan cheese, for serving
- Salt and pepper, to taste

Preparation time: 5 minutes
Cooking time: 15 minutes
Serves: 4

Directions:

1. In the inner pot of the pressure cooker, add all ingredients except for the cheese and stir to combine.
2. Close the lid completely and slide the pressure valve to locked position.
3. Press the "Beans/Lentils" button which automatically sets the pressure cooking time to 5 minutes.
4. When the pressure cooking cycle is completed, slide the pressure valve to open position to fully release the pressure. Open the lid when pressure has released.
5. Adjust seasonings if desired and transfer into a serving bowl or platter. Serve immediately with grated Parmesan on top.

GNOCCHI IN CHEESY ALFREDO SAUCE

Gnocchi may look and sound fancy, but there is no reason why it shouldn't have a place at your table. This recipe makes serving up this classic Italian dish easy with a few simple ingredients.

Ingredients:

- 1 pound spinach or potato gnocchi
- 1 ½ cups of three-cheese Alfredo sauce
- ½ cup chicken stock or water
- 1 cup shredded or chopped cooked chicken
- ½ cup sliced button mushrooms
- Salt and pepper, to taste

Preparation time: 5 minutes
Cooking time: 15 minutes
Serves: 4

Directions:

1. In the inner pot of the pressure cooker, combine together all ingredients and season to taste with salt and pepper. Stir to combine.
2. Close the lid completely and position pressure valve to locked position.
3. Press the "Beans/Lentils" button and which will automatically set the pressure cooking time to 5 minutes.
4. When the pressure cooking cycle is completed, slide the pressure valve to open position to fully release the pressure. Open the lid when pressure has released.
5. Adjust seasonings if desired, transfer into a serving bowl or platter and serve immediately.

Seafood

SHRIMP TIKKA MASALA

This is a simple and delicious dinner that any shrimp lover will enjoy. The tikka masala is a creamy, lightly spiced tomato broth that is a classic in Indian cuisine. The shrimp will be perfectly cooked in the flavorful sauce. Serve over rice for an easy, elegant meal.

Ingredients:

- 2 tablespoons clarified butter
- 1 teaspoon of minced garlic
- 1 cup jarred Tikka masala sauce
- 1 pound of fresh medium shrimp, peeled and deveined
- ½ cup coconut milk
- Salt and pepper, to taste

Preparation time: 10 minutes
Cooking time: 10 minutes
Serves: 4

Directions:

1. In the inner pot of the pressure cooker, add the butter and press the "Meat/Chicken" button. Sauté the garlic until fragrant and add in the shrimp and remaining ingredients. Season to taste with salt and pepper, stir to combine and press the "Keep Warm/Cancel" button.
2. Close the lid completely and slide the pressure valve to locked position.
3. Press the "Fish/Veg/Steam" button which will set the pressure cooking time to 2 minutes.
4. When the pressure cooking cycle is completed, slide the pressure valve to open position to fully release the pressure. Open the lid when pressure has released.
5. Adjust seasonings if desired, transfer to a serving bowl and serve immediately over rice.

CRAB CAKES WITH ROASTED PEPPER SAUCE

Crab cakes are delicious, but can be a bit of a pain to make, especially on busy nights. Frozen crab cakes cooked in a yummy sauce in the Power Pressure Cooker XL make a dinner everyone will enjoy with none of the hassle.

Ingredients:

- 4 pieces of packaged frozen crab cakes, thawed
- ½ cup jarred roasted red pepper and garlic sauce
- ½ cup of mayonnaise
- 1 tablespoon lemon juice
- 2 tablespoons of clarified butter
- ¼ cup water
- Salt and pepper, to taste

Preparation time: 5 minutes
Cooking time: 15 minutes
Serves: 4

Directions:

1. In the inner pot of the pressure cooker, add the butter and press the "Meat/Chicken" button. Fry the crab cake in melted butter for about 3 minutes on each side or until lightly browned.
2. Combine together the remaining ingredients in a bowl, pour into the inner pot and press the "Keep Warm/Cancel" button.
3. Close the lid completely and slide the pressure valve to locked position.
4. Press the "Beans/Lentils" button which sets cooking time to 5 minutes.
5. When the pressure cooking cycle is completed, slide the pressure valve to open position to fully release the pressure. Open the lid when pressure has released.
6. Adjust seasonings if desired, transfer to a serving platter and serve immediately.

CAJUN SHRIMP AND ASPARGUS

This healthy meal is sure to please everyone at the table. The steamed shrimp and asparagus are quite flavorful with the addition of the cajun seasonings. Adjust the spiciness by adding more or less of the seasoning and be sure to serve with a side of lemon.

Ingredients:

- 1 pound peeled and deveined fresh shrimp
- Package fresh asparagus, stalks trimmed
- 1-2 teaspoons olive oil
- 1/2 tablespoon Cajon seasoning, divided
- 1 cup water
- Lemon wedge for serving, optional

Preparation time: 5 minutes
Cooking time: 10 minutes
Serves: 4 to 6

Directions:

1. In the inner pot of the pressure cooker, add the water and insert the steamer tray.
2. Place the trimmed asparagus on the steamer tray and sprinkle with a light dusting of the Cajun seasoning.
3. Toss the shrimp, olive oil and the remainder of the Cajun seasoning so the shrimp is well coated. Place it on top of the asparagus.
4. Close the lid completely and slide the pressure valve to locked position.
5. Press the "Fish/Veg/Steam" button which selects pressure cooking time of 2 minutes.
6. When the pressure cooking cycle is completed, slide the pressure valve to open position to fully release the pressure. Open the lid when pressure has released.
7. Adjust seasonings if desired, transfer to a serving platter and serve immediately with a lemon wedge.

MAHI MAHI IN GREEN CHILE SAUCE

This steamed Mahi Mahi is made even more enjoyable by being covered in a yummy green enchilada sauce, adding so much flavor and that you will never believe you cooked it all in your pressure cooker.

Ingredients:

- 2 thawed Mahi Mahi fillets
- sprinkle of garlic powder
- 1/4 cup jarred or homemade green enchilada sauce
- 1-2 teaspoons olive oil
- 2 cups water
- salt and pepper, to taste

Preparation time: 5 minutes
Cooking time: 10 minutes
Serves: 4 to 6

Directions:

1. In the inner pot of the pressure cooker, add the water and insert the steamer tray.
2. Spread olive oil on the bottom of the fish to prevent it from sticking to the steam rack. Season the fish with garlic powder, salt and pepper. Place it on the steamer tray in the pressure cooker.
3. Top the fish with the green enchilada sauce, making sure to cover the entire length of the fish.
4. Close the lid completely and slide the pressure valve to locked position.
5. Press the "Fish/Veg/Steam" button and use "Cook Time Selector" button to set the pressure cooking time to 4 minutes.
6. When the pressure cooking cycle is completed, slide the pressure valve to open position to fully release the pressure. Open the lid when pressure has released.
7. Carefully remove the steam rack and transfer the fish to a serving platter. Adjust seasonings if desired and serve immediately.

WHITE FISH IN TAMARIND BROTH

This Fillipino dish is a heavy hitter when it comes to taste and flavor. Its quite simple to prepare and can use any variety of white fish that you find at your grocery store. You can vary the intensity of the heat by adding more or less of the jalepeno peppers.

Ingredients:

- 2 to 3 pounds white fish of your choice, sliced into serving sizes (example, cod, haddock or trout)
- 1 packet of tamarind seasoning mix or soup base
- 4 cups of fish stock or vegetable broth
- 1 cup diced tomatoes
- 2 jalapeno peppers, stalk removed
- Salt and pepper, to taste

Preparation time: 10 minutes
Cooking time: 20 minutes
Serves: 4 to 6

Directions:

1. In the inner pot of the pressure cooker, add all ingredients and season to taste with salt and pepper.
2. Close the lid completely and slide the pressure valve to locked position.
3. Press the "Soup/Stew" button which will automatically set the pressure cooking time to 10 minutes.
4. When the pressure cooking cycle is completed, slide the pressure valve to open position to fully release the pressure. Open the lid when pressure has released.
5. Adjust seasonings if desired, transfer into a serving bowl and serve immediately.

HERBED GARLIC SALMON FILLET

Salmon steams perfectly in the Power Pressure Cooker XL. The herbed garlic cream sauce is light and flavorful and absolutely delicious with the fish.

Ingredients:

- 2 fresh salmon fillets
- ½ cup garlic and herb butter or homemade compound butter with garlic and herbs
- Salt and pepper, to taste
- 2 tablespoons white wine
- ¼ cup cream
- 1 teaspoon lemon zest
- 2 cups water

Preparation time: *10 minutes*
Cooking time: *15 minutes*
Serves: *2*

Directions:

1. In the inner pot of the pressure cooker, add 2 cups of water and the steamer tray. Place the fish, skin side down on the steamer tray and season, to taste.
2. Close the lid completely and slide the pressure valve to locked position.
3. Press the "Beans/ Lentils" button which will automatically set the pressure cooking time to 5 minutes.
4. When the pressure cooking cycle is completed, slide the pressure valve to open position to fully release the pressure. Open the lid when pressure has released.
5. Remove the fish and cover to keep warm. Remove the steamer tray and drain the water. Place the inner pot back in the pressure cooker and press the "Meat/Chicken" button. Melt the garlic butter. Stir in the wine and cook until bubbling. Stir in the cream and top with the lemon zest. Mix well and cook until warm.
6. Transfer salmon to serving plates. Top with the creamy sauce and serve.

Beef

MEATBALLS IN TOMATO-BASIL SAUCE

Making your own meatballs is actually very simple and just requires a few minutes of your time. This very basic recipe is delicious, but also easy to add your own spin, if you'd like. I like pressure cooking the meatballs in the sauce as it really adds so much flavor to both the meatballs and the sauce. Serve over your favorite cooked pasta.

Ingredients:

- 2 cups of jarred tomato with basil and garlic sauce
- 1 pound of ground beef (80% lean/20% fat)
- 1 large egg
- ¼ Italian Seasoned Breadcrumbs
- ½ cup of beef broth
- 1 cup of diced white onion
- Salt and black pepper, to taste
- Drizzle of olive oil

Preparation time: 20 minutes
Cooking time: 45 minutes
Serves: 4

Directions:

1. Season the ground beef with salt and pepper, stir in the egg and breadcrumbs and mix to combine. Divide into 8 equal portions and form into balls.
2. In the inner pot of the pressure cooker, add the oil and press the "Meat/Chicken" button. Add the meatballs and cook until evenly browned on all sides while turning occasionally. Stir in the onions, cook until soft and tender and pour in the tomato sauce. Bring to a boil, add in the broth and stir to combine. If sauce appears too thick, add a bit more broth. Press the "Keep Warm/Cancel" button.
3. Close the lid completely and slide the pressure valve to locked position.
4. Press the "Meat/Chicken" button and set the pressure cooking time to 15 minutes.
5. When the pressure cooking cycle is completed, allow the pressure to release naturally for 15 minutes. Open the lid when pressure has released.
6. Adjust seasonings if desired, transfer to a serving bowl and serve immediately over pasta.

BEEF STROGANOFF

The first time I made beef stroganoff in the Power Pressure Cooker XL I was blown away at how tender the meat became. Years of preparing this dish and I'd never had meat so tender! This is a creamy, lovely dish that is delicious over egg noodles and sure to please everyone at your table.

Ingredients:

- 1 ½ pounds of thinly sliced sirloin
- 1 small onion, diced
- 1 cup fresh mushrooms, sliced
- 1 ½ cup of beef broth
- 3 tablespoons flour
- ½ cup sour cream
- salt and pepper, or preferred seasoning
- olive oil

Preparation time: **20** *minutes*
Cooking time: **40** *minutes*
Serves: **4-6**

Directions:

1. In the inner pot of the pressure cooker, add the oil and press the "Meat/Chicken" button. Season the beef with salt and pepper and add to the inner pot. Brown the beef lightly, then add the onions and mushrooms. Cook until soft and translucent.
2. Pour the beef broth into the inner pot and stir, being sure to scrape any browned bits from the bottom of the pan. Stir to combine and press the "Keep Warm/Cancel" button.
3. Close the lid completely and slide the pressure valve to locked position.
4. Press the "Meat/Chicken" button and use "Time Adjuster" feature to set the pressure cooking time to 20 minutes.
5. While the beef is cooking, stir together the sour cream and flour.
6. When the pressure cooking cycle is completed, slide the pressure valve to open position to fully release the pressure. Open the lid when pressure has released. Press the "Keep Warm/Cancel" button.
7. Stir the sour cream mixture into the beef, check taste, adding more sour cream or seasonings if you desire. If you want a thicker sauce, press the "Meat/Chicken" button and simmer in "Meat/Chicken" mode until you reach the desired consistency.
8. Serve immediately over cooked egg noodles.

BEEF BBQ

This delicious meat is sure to make a memorable meal. The sauce is light, yet flavorful and the meat is super easy to shred with a fork. Serve on its own or with some buns with a side of your favorite barbecue sauce for those that like their barbecue extra saucy!

Ingredients:

- 3 pound chuck roast
- 1 (6 ounce) can tomato paste
- 2 tablespoons mustard
- 2 tablespoons dried minced onion
- 1 teaspoon garlic powder
- 2 tablespoons apple cider vinegar
- Salt and pepper, 1 teaspoon of each
- drizzle olive oil
- water

Preparation time: 15 minutes
Cooking time: 1 hour, 30 minutes
Serves: 6

Directions:

1. In the inner pot of the pressure cooker, press the "Meat/Chicken" button and add a drizzle of olive oil. Add the beef and brown evenly on all sides. Transfer to a plate when completely browned and press the "Keep Warm/Cancel" button.
2. Add the tomato paste, mustard, salt, pepper, dried onion, garlic powder, and vinegar to the inner pot. Pour in enough water to just reach the 2 cup line on the pot. Stir well and then add the beef back to the pot.
3. Close the lid completely and slide the pressure valve to locked position.
4. Press the "Meat/Chicken" button and press "Cook Time Selector" button twice to set the pressure cooking time to 60 minutes.
5. When the pressure cooking cycle is completed, allow the pressure to release naturally. Open the lid when pressure has released.
6. Shred meat on a separate plate then add the meat back to the pot to soak in the juices. Serve warm with additional bbq sauce, if desired. This recipe is wonderful served just as it is, or on buns.

BEEF CURRY

I've recently discovered a wonderful jarred tikka masala at our grocery store that my family loves. This sauce helps me make this delicious beef curry that my whole family enjoys. Its a simple and healthy weeknight meal that I can get everyone to eat.

Ingredients:

- 1 ½ cups jarred tikka masala or madras curry sauce
- 1 ½ pounds of beef chuck steak (trimmed to ¼" fat), cut into cubes
- 1 cup beef broth
- ½ cup coconut milk
- Salt and pepper, to taste
- Optional toppings (sliced green chilis, chopped coriander or basil leaves)

Preparation time: 15 minutes
Cooking time: 40 minutes
Serves: 4 to 6

Directions:

1. Season the beef with salt and pepper.
2. In the inner pot of the pressure cooker, press the "Meat/Chicken" button and add the beef. Cook until evenly browned on all sides. Stir in the remaining ingredients and mix until well combined. Press the "Keep Warm/Cancel" button.
3. Close the lid completely and slide the pressure valve to locked position.
4. Press the "Rice/Risotto" button and press "Cook Time Selector" button twice to automatically set the pressure cooking time to 25 minutes.
5. When the pressure cooking cycle is completed, slide the pressure valve to open position to fully release the pressure. Open the lid when pressure has released.
6. Serve over rice with any additional toppings you desire.

CHIPOTLE BEEF BARBECUE BRISKET

Brisket can be a tough cut of meat to master. If not cooked properly you wind up a chewy, tough hunk of meat and a disappointed crowd. There will be no disappointment with this recipe, though. The Power Pressure Cooker XL produces savory, juicy brisket every time.

Ingredients:

- 3 pounds beef brisket,
- 2 cups of chipotle barbecue sauce
- ¼ cup of brown sugar
- 2 tablespoons of Worcestershire sauce
- 2 tablespoons apple cider vinegar
- ½ -1 cup beef stock

Preparation time: 10 minutes
Cooking time:
1 hour, 15 minutes
Serves: 6 to 8

Directions:

1. In the inner pot of the pressure cooker, add the beef and press the "Meat/Chicken" button. Cook until the beef is evenly browned on all sides and add in the remaining ingredients. Stir to combine, bring to a boil and press the "Keep Warm/Cancel" button.
2. Close the lid completely and slide the pressure valve to locked position.
3. Press the "Meat/Chicken" button and use "Time Adjustment" button to set the pressure cooking time to 50 minutes.
4. When the pressure cooking cycle is completed, allow the pressure to release naturally for 10 minutes. Slide the pressure valve to open position to fully release the pressure. Open the lid when pressure has released. Cook further if the sauce is not yet thick using the "Meat/Chicken" function until the desired consistency is achieved.
5. Transfer to a serving platter, slice and serve immediately.

ITALIAN SHREDDED BEEF

This is the meat typically used in Italian Beef sandwiches. Its super easy, shreds with a fork and has so much flavor! To make the sandwiches, use hoagie rolls and provolone cheese. Top the rolls with the cheese and healthy helping of the shredded beef. Add extra peppers if your little heart desires and toast lightly in the oven, until the cheese just starts to melt. Hope you enjoy!

Ingredients:

- 2 tablespoons olive oil
- 3 pound beef chuck roast
- 2 tablespoons of minced garlic
- 12 ounce jar pepperoncini
- 2 cups beef broth
- Salt and pepper, to taste

Preparation time: 15 minutes
Cooking time:
1 hour, 10 minutes
Serves: 8

Directions:

1. Season the beef with salt and pepper, set aside.
2. In the inner pot of the pressure cooker, add the oil and press the "Meat/Chicken" button. Add the beef and cook until it is evenly seared on all sides and stir in the garlic. Saute until lightly brown, then press the "Keep Warm/Cancel" button.
3. Cut the stems off of the pepperoncini. Make sure to reserve half of the juice. Add reserved juice, peppers and broth to the inner pot.
4. Close the lid completely and slide the pressure valve to locked position.
5. Press the "Meat/Chicken" button and use "Time Adjustment" button to set the pressure cooking time to 45 minutes.
6. When the pressure cooking cycle is completed,allow the pressure to release naturally for about 10 minutes. Then slide the pressure valve to open position to fully release the pressure and open the lid when pressure has released.
7. Remove beef and shred. The juices from the meat can be reserved for dipping or pouring on the shredded meat. Serve immediately.

EASY POT ROAST

Pot Roast for dinner anyone? The Power Pressure Cooker XL has taken the guesswork out of cooking the pot roast, which if overcooked can be bland and dry. The onion soup mix adds so much flavor, to both the meat and the gravy. Use a homemade version of cream of mushroom soup of you prefer.

Ingredients:

- 4 pound chuck roast,
- 1 (10.25 ounce) can cream of mushroom soup
- 1 envelope beefy onion soup mix
- 2 onions, sliced into rounds
- 2 cups beef broth, low sodium
- drizzle olive oil

Preparation time: 15 minutes
Cooking time:
1 hour, 25 minutes
Serves: 4

Directions:

1. In the inner pot of the pressure cooker, add the olive oil and press the "Meat/Chicken" button. Use the beefy onion soup mix to season the meat all over. Add the roast to the inner pot and sear lightly on all sides. Remove the meat and set aside.
2. Pour the broth into the pot and use a spatula to scrape any browned bits off the bottom of the pot. Add the onions and place the meat on top of the onions. Pour the cream of mushroom soup on top of the roast. Press the "Keep Warm/Cancel" button.
3. Close the lid completely and slide the pressure valve to locked position.
4. Press the "Meat/Chicken" button and use "Time Adjustment" button to set the pressure cooking time to 45 minutes.
5. When the pressure cooking cycle is completed, allow the pressure to release naturally until the float valve has dropped.
6. Transfer to a serving platter. Thicken gravy if desired and serve over the top of the roast.

BBQ SHORT RIBS

Short ribs are so delicious and so easy, yet when I serve them to my family, I feel like I am serving us something special. Thats probably because they are so tender and flavorful and everyone loves them. This easy recipe is sure to make your family feel like they are loved!

Ingredients:

- 4 pounds beef short ribs
- 1 onion, diced
- 2 cups barbecue sauce
- 2 tablespoons honey
- 1 tablespoon Dijon mustard
- 1/2 can beer
- salt, pepper or seasonings of your choice
- drizzle olive oil

Preparation time: 25 minutes
Cooking time: 55 minutes
Serves: 6

Directions:

1. In the inner pot of the pressure cooker, add the oil and press the "Meat/Chicken" button. Season the short ribs liberally with the seasoning of your preference. Add them to the inner pot, allowing them to brown lightly on both sides, working in batches if necessary. When all ribs are browned, remove from the pot and place on a plate.

2. Add the onions to the pot and cook until soft and fragrant.

3. While onions are cooking, mix together the barbecue sauce, mustard, honey and beer. When onions are soft, add the ribs back to the pot, on top of the onions. Pour the liquid mixture over the ribs. Press the "Keep Warm/Cancel" button.

4. Close the lid completely and slide the pressure valve to locked position.

5. Press the "Meat/Chicken" button and use "Time Adjustment" button to set the pressure cooking time to 35 minutes.

6. When the pressure cooking cycle is completed allow the pressure to release naturally for 5 minutes. Then slide the pressure valve to open position to fully release the pressure. Open the lid when pressure has released.

7. Transfer to a serving platter and serve immediately topped with extra sauce from the pot.

MEATLOAF

A simple, timeless classic. Meatloaf might be the ultimate comfort food. And this recipe has added a bit of cheese, making it in instant favorite. This is a basic, but tasty recipe that cooks right on the steamer tray in your Power Pressure Cooker XL. Feel free to add your choice of seasonings.

Ingredients:

- 2 pounds of ground beef
- 3 large eggs
- 1 ½ cups Panko bread crumbs
- 1 cup shredded Parmesan cheese
- 1 tablespoon Worcestershire sauce
- ½ cup ketchup
- 2 cups water
- salt and pepper, to taste

Preparation time: 10 minutes
Cooking time: 50 minutes
Serves: 6

Directions:

1. Combine together the ground beef, egg, Panko, cheese, and Worcestershire sauce in a bowl and season lightly with salt and pepper. Mix until well combined and form into a loaf that will fit in the inner pot.
2. Add 2 cups of water to the inner pot. Place you steamer tray in the pot and rest the formed meat loaf on top. Coat the top of the loaf with the ketchup.
3. Close the lid completely and slide the pressure valve to locked position.
4. Press the "Meat/Chicken" button and use the "Time Adjustment" button to set the pressure cooking time to 35 minutes.
5. When the pressure cooking cycle is completed, slide the pressure valve to open position to fully release the pressure. Open the lid when pressure has released.
6. Check to be sure meatloaf is cooked through, cooking in 3-5 minute intervals if it needs more cooking time. Transfer to a serving platter and serve immediately.

BEEF STRIPS IN AU JUS GRAVY

This is a great week night meal that can be eaten just as it is or use the meat to prepare au jus sandwiches. The flank steak will be nice and tender and the au jus sauce is will be ready to go.

Ingredients:

- 1 ½ cups of canned/jarred au jus gravy
- 1 ½ pounds of beef sirloin or flank steak, sliced into strips
- 1 tablespoon of oil
- 1 teaspoon Italian seasoning mix
- ½ cup of beef broth
- Salt and pepper, to taste

Preparation time: 5 minutes
Cooking time: 25 minutes
Serves: 6

Directions:

1. In the inner pot of the pressure cooker, add the oil and press the "Meat/Chicken" button. Season the beef with salt and pepper and add into the inner pot. Cook until evenly browned on all sides and add in the remaining ingredients. Stir to combine and press the "Keep Warm/Cancel" button.
2. Close the lid completely and slide the pressure valve to locked position.
3. Press the "Meat/Chicken" button and which will automatically set the pressure cooking time to 15 minutes.
4. When the pressure cooking cycle is completed, slide the pressure valve to open position to fully release the pressure. Open the lid when pressure has released.
5. Adjust seasoning if desired, transfer to a serving bowl or platter and serve immediately.

SLOPPY JOES

This is a classic family pleaser that has had an Power Pressure Cooker XL makeover! If you prefer not to use a pre-packaged seasoning, feel free to use your own spice mix. You can also add a little grated carrots to sneak in some veggies for the kids.

Ingredients:

- 2 pounds ground beef (80% lean/20% fat)
- 2 packets Sloppy Joe Seasoning (McCormick)
- 1 tablespoon minced garlic
- 1 onion, diced
- 1 (15 ounce) can diced tomatoes
- 1 (6 ounce) can tomato paste
- Salt and pepper, to taste
- 1 ¼ water

Preparation time: 15 minutes
Cooking time: 20 minutes
Serves: 8

Directions:

1. In the inner pot of the pressure cooker, add the beef and press the "Meat/Chicken" button. Season to with salt and pepper and cook until mostly browned. Push the beef on one side of the inner pot and add in the onion and garlic. Sauté until soft and fragrant and stir in the remaining ingredients. Stir to combine and press the "Keep Warm/Cancel" button.
2. Close the lid completely and slide the pressure valve to locked position.
3. Press the "Soup/Stew" button which automatically sets the pressure cooking time to 10 minutes.
4. When the pressure cooking cycle is completed, slide the pressure valve to open position to fully release the pressure. Open the lid when pressure has released.
5. Adjust seasonings if desired, transfer to a serving bowl and serve immediately on buns or rolls.

CRANBERRY BEEF BRISKET

This is a very tasty meal that is certainly worth serving to guests, even if it does include only a few ingredients! The onion soup mix provides great flavor and the cranberry sauce gives it a beautiful presentation.

Ingredients:

- 3-4 pound beef brisket
- 1 can whole-berry cranberry sauce
- 1 (12 ounce) can ginger ale
- ½ cup dried cranberries
- 1 packet onion soup mix
- salt and pepper, to taste
- drizzle olive oil

Preparation time: 15 minutes
Cooking time:
1 hour, 15 minutes
Serves: 6

Directions:

1. In the inner pot of the pressure cooker, add a drizzle of oil and press the "Meat/Chicken" button. Lightly season the brisket with salt and pepper and add it to the inner pot. Brown the brisket lightly on all sides.
2. While brisket is browning, stir together the remaining ingredients in a separate bowl. When meat is ready, add the liquid mixture to the inner pot. Stir to combine and press the "Keep Warm/Cancel" button.
3. Close the lid completely and slide the pressure valve to locked position.
4. Press the "Meat/Chicken" button and use "Time Adjustment" button to set the pressure cooking time to 50 minutes.
5. When the pressure cooking cycle is completed, slide the pressure valve to open position to fully release the pressure. Open the lid when pressure has released.
6. Adjust seasonings if desired, transfer to a serving platter and serve immediately.

BEEF AND BROCCOLI

The recipe is a sure bet for getting everyone to eat a little healthy broccoli. You can play with the recipe according to your family's taste. Add more sauce if you like, but be sure to add a little more beef broth so it isn't so thick that the Power Pressure Cooker XL won't come to pressure. If you like your broccoli a little more cooked, pressure cook for an additional minute.

Ingredients:

- 1 pound of beef, cut into strips
- 1 cup jarred stir-fry sauce
- 1 small onion, diced
- 1 tablespoon minced garlic
- ½-1 cup beef broth
- 4-5 cups broccoli florets
- Salt and pepper, to taste
- drizzle cooking oil

Preparation time: 10 minutes
Cooking time: 20 minutes
Serves: 4 to 6

Directions:

1. In the inner pot of the pressure cooker, add the oil and press the "Meat/Chicken" button. Season the beef with salt and pepper and cook until evenly browned on all sides. Add in the onions and cook until soft and fragrant. Stir in the garlic and cook for one minute more.
2. Mix the beef broth and the stir-fry sauce together and pour over the beef and onion mixture. Press the "Keep Warm/Cancel" button.
3. Close the lid completely and slide the pressure valve to locked position.
4. Press the "Soup/Stew" button which will set the pressure cooking time to 10 minutes.
5. When the pressure cooking cycle is completed, slide the pressure valve to open position to fully release the pressure. Open the lid when pressure has released.
6. Add the broccoli florets to the pot. Close the lid and secure the slide pressure valve to locked position. Press the "Fish/Veg/Steam button which sets the timer for 2 minutes.
7. When cooking time is completed, perform a quick release of the pressure and open the lid.
8. Mix the broccoli into the beef and sauce mixture. Adjust seasonings if desired, transfer to a serving bowl and serve immediately.

CHILI BARBECUE STEAKS

Even a typically tough cut of meat is no match for the Power Pressure Cooker XL. These steaks will be so tender and have great flavor. Be sure to serve with the remaining sauce on the side.

Ingredients:

- 2 cups hot and spicy barbecue sauce
- 1 teaspoon of BBQ rub
- 2 pounds beef top sirloin steaks
- ½ cup beef broth
- 2 tablespoons Worcestershire sauce
- 2 tablespoons of brown sugar

Preparation time: 10 minutes
Cooking time: 40 minutes
Serves: 6 to 8

Directions:

1. Season the beef with BBQ rub on both sides. Combine together beef broth, barbecue sauce, sugar and Worcestershire sauce in a bowl and set aside.
2. In the inner pot of the pressure cooker, add the press the "Meat/Chicken" button and add the beef. Cook until evenly seared on both sides. Pour in the BBQ sauce, stir to combine and press the "Keep Warm/Cancel" button.
3. Close the lid completely and slide the pressure valve to locked position.
4. Press the "Rice/Risotto" button and use "Cook Time Selector" feature twice to set the pressure cooking time to 25 minutes.
5. When the pressure cooking cycle is completed, slide the pressure valve to open position to fully release the pressure. Open the lid when pressure has released.
6. Adjust seasonings if desired and stir to evenly coat the meat with sauce. Transfer to a serving platter and serve immediately.

BEEF IN CREAMY MUSHROOM SAUCE

The Power Pressure Cooker XL must work hard to get the stew meat so tender! Use any Alfredo or white cream sauce that you prefer. I often make this with onions and mushrooms, but play around and add other vegetables that you like. I think adding spinach at the end would be a great way to add a little green to your meal!

Ingredients:

- 2 ½ cups Alfredo sauce (mushroom Alfredo if you can find it)
- 1 teaspoon Italian seasoning mix
- 1 ½ pounds of beef stew meat
- 1 cup diced onion
- 1 cup button mushrooms, halved
- ½ cup beef broth
- Salt and pepper, to taste

Preparation time: 15 minutes
Cooking time: 30 minutes
Serves: 6

Directions:

1. In the inner pot of the pressure cooker, add the beef and season with salt and pepper. Press the "Meat/Chicken" button, cook until evenly browned on all sides and stir in the onions and mushrooms. Cook until the mushrooms and onions are soft.
2. Add in the remaining ingredients and stir to combine. Press the "Keep Warm/Cancel" button.
3. Close the lid completely and position the pressure valve to the locked position.
4. Press the "Meat/Chicken" button and use "Time Adjustment" button to set the pressure cooking time to 20 minutes.
5. When the pressure cooking cycle is completed, slide the pressure valve to open position to fully release the pressure. Open the lid when pressure has released.
6. Adjust seasonings and consistency if desired by using the "Meat/Chicken" feature to lightly boil sauce to desired thickness. Transfer to a serving bowl and serve immediately over egg noodles or mashed potatoes.

SWEET AND SAVORY MEATBALLS

These meatballs are a staple at any large gathering we host and always for our New Year's Eve party. I like that they don't have to be prepared ahead of time and they are hands-off after they are in the pot. We've even been known to eat these as a meal, with a side of mashed potatoes.

Ingredients:

- 1 package frozen meatballs (64 ounces) or 3-4 pounds pre-cooked homemade meatballs
- 1 cup grape jelly
- 1 cup apple jelly
- 1 cup ketchup
- 1 (8 ounce) can tomato sauce

Preparation time: 10 minutes
Cooking time: 25 minutes
Serves: 4

Directions:

1. In the inner pot of the pressure cooker, press the "Meat/Chicken" button and add the ketchup, tomato sauce, apple and grape jelly. Simmer and whisk until all ingredients are combined.
2. Gently stir in the meatballs, coating with the sauce. Press the "Keep Warm/Cancel" button.
3. Close the lid completely and slide the pressure valve to locked position.
4. Press the "Beans/Lentils" button which automatically sets the pressure cooking time to 5 minutes.
5. When the pressure cooking cycle is completed, allow pressure to release naturally for about 10 minutes then slide the pressure valve to open position to fully release the pressure. Open the lid when pressure has released.
6. Transfer to a serving dish and serve warm with toothpicks.

SPAGHETTI WITH CHUNKY TOMATO MEAT SAUCE

I was a bit dubious before trying pressure cooker spaghetti, thinking why go through the trouble if the noodles are already prepared? But this spaghetti is incredibly good! The beef and onion all cook in the pot, then add the remaining ingredients for a simple and delicious meal.

Ingredients:

- 3 cups of cooked spaghetti
- 1 pound of ground beef (80% lean/20% fat)
- 1 cup diced white onion
- 2 ½ cups of canned/jarred seasoned tomato sauce
- ½ cup beef broth
- ½ cup grated Parmesan cheese
- Salt and pepper, to taste

Preparation time: 15 minutes
Cooking time: 25 minutes
Serves: 4 to 6

Directions:

1. In the inner pot of the pressure cooker, add the ground meat and press the "Meat/Chicken" button. Cook until browned evenly, push to one side and stir in the onions. Season to taste with salt and pepper, cook until the onion is soft and pour in the tomato sauce.
2. Stir to combine and press the "Keep Warm/Cancel" button.
3. Close the lid completely and slide the pressure valve to locked position.
4. Press the "Meat/Chicken" button and set the pressure cooking time to 15 minutes.
5. When the pressure cooking cycle is completed, slide the pressure valve to open position to fully release the pressure. Open the lid when pressure has released.
6. Add in the cooked spaghetti and toss to coat evenly with sauce. Adjust seasonings if desired, transfer to a serving bowl and serve with grated Parmesan cheese on top.

SAUCY SHREDDED BEEF

This easy meal has great flavor and can be served in a variety of ways. Some in my family like to eat it just as it is, some prefer it on a bun and I like it served over a piece of white bread. Be sure to serve with the juices, it adds so much flavor!

Ingredients:

- 2-3 pound chuck roast
- 1 packet Italian Dressing Seasoning mix
- 1 packet Au Jus gravy mix
- 1 cup beef broth
- drizzle of oil

Preparation time: *10* minutes
Cooking time:
1 hour, 10 minutes
Serves: *4*

Directions:

1. In the inner pot of the pressure cooker, press the "Meat/Chicken" button and add the oil. Sear the chuck roast evenly on all sides.
2. In a separate bowl, mix together the remaining ingredients. When roast is lightly browned, add the broth mixture to the inner pot. Press the "Keep Warm/Cancel" button.
3. Close the lid completely and slide the pressure valve to locked position.
4. Press the "Meat/Chicken" button and use "Time Adjustment" button to set the pressure cooking time to 45 minutes.
5. When the pressure cooking cycle is completed, allow the pressure to release naturally for 10 minutes. Then slide the pressure valve to open position to fully release the pressure. Open the lid when pressure has released.
6. Adjust seasonings if desired, transfer to a serving bowl to shred further if desired. Serve by itself or on buns with remaining liquid as a dipping sauce.

CORNED BEEF

Corned Beef is essentially salt-cured beef and gets its name from the large grains of salt, called corns, that are used to treat the meat. Corned beef can be found in your grocery store and is easy to fix in the Power Pressure Cooker XL. For traditional corned been and cabbage, cut a cabbage into six pieces. When the beef is done cooking and removed from the pot, place cabbage into the liquid and cook for 3-5 minutes using the "Fish/Veg/Steam" button.

Ingredients:

- 3 pounds of flat cut corned beef brisket with spice packet, cut into two portions
- 2 garlic cloves, crushed
- 1 tablespoon apple cider vinegar
- 1 bay leaf
- 1 teaspoon Italian seasoning mix
- Beef broth, as needed to cover the meat

Preparation time: 5 minutes
Cooking time: 50 minutes
Serves: 8

Directions:

1. In the inner pot of the pressure cooker, add all ingredients except for the meat and stir to combine. Add the corned beef and pour in more broth if needed to cover the meat completely.
2. Close the lid completely and slide the pressure valve to locked position.
3. Press the "Meat/Chicken" button and use "Time Adjustment" button to set the pressure cooking time to 30 minutes.
4. When the pressure cooking cycle is completed, let all of the pressure release naturally. Open the lid when pressure has released.
5. Transfer to a serving platter and let it rest for about 10 minutes. Thinly slice the meat across the grain and serve immediately.

CHIPOTLE BEEF POT ROAST

I want to love spicy foods, but unfortunately my mouth doesn't always agree with me. This Chipotle Pot Roast has great flavor but is not too spicy, so that even those with mild palates will enjoy it. The Power Pressure Cooker XL helps to create a juicy, tender cut of meat.

Ingredients:

- 1 cup diced onions
- 3 pounds of beef chuck roast
- 2 cups of beef broth
- 1 cup diced tomatoes
- 2 chipotle peppers in adobo sauce, drained and chopped
- Salt and black pepper, to taste

Preparation time: 10 minutes
Cooking time:
1 hour, 10 minutes
Serves: 6

Directions:

1. Place the onions and tomatoes in the inner pot of the pressure cooker, spread evenly on the bottom of the inner pot and place the beef chuck roast on top. Pour in the broth, place the chipotle peppers on top of the meat and season to taste with salt and pepper.
2. Close the lid completely and slide the pressure valve to locked position.
3. Press the "Meat/Chicken" button and use the "Time Adjustment" feature to set the pressure cooking time to 45 minutes.
4. When the pressure cooking cycle is completed, slide the pressure valve to open position to fully release the pressure. Open the lid when pressure has released.
5. Turn the beef to coat the other side in the sauce mixture and adjust seasonings if desired. Transfer to a cutting board. Let it rest for about 10 minutes and shred or slice the beef roast.
6. Serve immediately with sauce drizzled on top.

chicken

CHICKEN ADOBO

This Filipino dish is widely known and is essentially chicken stewed in soy sauce and vinegar. The result is a juicy chicken dish that is full of flavor. The Power Pressure Cooker XL insures that your chicken won't be overcooked, as is a concern when making this in more traditional ways.

Ingredients:

- 4 pounds chicken legs and thighs, bone-in
- ½ cup Tamari soy sauce
- 1 ½ teaspoons of black peppercorns (1 teaspoon whole and ½ teaspoon crushed)
- 4 garlic cloves, crushed
- 2 bay leaves
- 1/3 cup apple cider vinegar
- drizzle olive oil

Preparation time: 10 minutes
Cooking time: 25 minutes
Serves: 4 to 6

Directions:

1. Combine the soy sauce, vinegar, ½ teaspoon crushed peppercorn, and bay leaves in a large bowl and add in the chicken. Toss to evenly coat the chicken with the soy sauce mixture and marinate it for at least 1 to 2 hours.
2. In the inner pot of the pressure cooker, add the oil and press the "Meat/Chicken" button. Add the garlic and remaining peppercorn and sauté until lightly browned and fragrant. Add in the chicken together with the marinade and press the "Keep Warm/Cancel" button.
3. Close the lid completely and slide the pressure valve to locked position.
4. Press the "Soup/Stew" button and use "Time Adjustment" feature to set the pressure cooking time to 12 minutes.
5. When the pressure cooking cycle is completed, slide the pressure valve to open position to fully release the pressure. Open the lid when pressure has released and gently stir to evenly distribute the ingredients. Thicken the sauce, if desired.
6. Transfer to a serving bowl or platter and serve immediately.

CHICKEN PROSCIUTTO ROLLS

This is a delicious that looks like slaved away in the kitchen, when in reality very little prep time is involved. Flatten all the chicken breast with a mallet so they are of comparable thickness and can cook equally throughout.

Ingredients:

- 6 chicken breast fillets, pounded thin
- 6 thin slices of prosciutto ham
- 1 ½ teaspoons of poultry seasoning mix
- 1 cup jarred Alfredo sauce
- 1 teaspoon minced garlic
- 2-3 tablespoons white wine (optional)
- Salt and black pepper, to taste
- drizzle olive oil

Preparation time: 20 minutes
Cooking time: 20 minutes
Serves: 6

Directions:

1. Season the flattened chicken breast with poultry seasoning, salt and pepper. Place a slice of ham on each flattened chicken breast and roll it upward. Secure with a toothpick.
2. In the inner pot of the pressure cooker, pour in the oil and press the "Meat/Chicken" button. Arrange the chicken rolls on the bottom of the pot and brown lightly on all sides. Remove from the pot when browned.
3. Use the white wine to deglaze the pot. Scrape at all the browned bits. Add the garlic and cook for one minute. Pour in the Alfredo sauce and stir to combine. Press the "Keep Warm/Cancel" button.
4. Add the chicken back to the pot in the cream sauce. Close the lid completely and slide the pressure valve to locked position.
5. Press the "Soup/ Stew" button which will automatically set the pressure cooking time to 10 minutes.
6. When the pressure cooking cycle is completed, slide the pressure valve to open position to fully release the pressure. Open the lid when pressure has released. Gently stir to evenly distribute the ingredients.
7. Adjust seasonings if desired, transfer to a serving platter and serve immediately.

STICKY GARLICKY CHICKEN

The kids love this recipe, although I do go a little easy on the peppercorns if I know I am cooking just for the kids. The sticky sauce will have you licking your fingers, its so good!

Ingredients:

- 3/4 cup honey
- 1/ 2 cup soy sauce
- 3 pounds of chicken thighs, boneless
- 1 teaspoon of crushed peppercorns
- 2 bay leaves
- 8 garlic cloves, crushed
- 1/2 cup water or chicken broth, as needed
- drizzle olive oil

Preparation time: 15 minutes
Cooking time: 25 minutes
Serves: 4 to 6

Directions:

1. Combine together the honey, soy sauce, crushed pepper, bay leaves, 4 garlic cloves and chicken and marinate it for at least 1 to 2 hours.
2. In the inner pot of the pressure cooker, add the oil and press the "Meat/Chicken" button. Add the remaining garlic and sauté until lightly brown and fragrant. Drain the chicken, reserving the marinade and add chicken into the inner pot. Cook chicken until evenly browned on both sides. Add the marinade mixture back to the pot, thinning with water or broth if necessary. Briefly stir to combine and press the "Keep Warm/Cancel" button.
3. Close the lid completely and slide the pressure valve to locked position.
4. Press the "Soup/Stew" button which automatically sets the pressure cooking time to 10 minutes.
5. When the pressure cooking cycle is completed, slide the pressure valve to open position to fully release the pressure. Open the lid when pressure has released, gently stir to evenly coat the chicken with the sauce and discard the bay leaves.
6. Transfer the chicken on a serving platter, drizzle with sauce and serve immediately.

CHICKEN WITH WHITE CREAM SAUCE

One of my favorite dishes as a kid was a chicken with mushrooms in a cream sauce that my mom would prepare. This is an easy way to make this comfort food in the Power Pressure Cooker XL. You can try lots of different things to vary the flavor of the sauce. Sometimes I will add a few tablespoons of white wine or a heavy sprinkle of paprika for both color and flavor. Just prepared as it is, I think your family will love the flavor of this dish.

Ingredients:

- 2 pounds chicken breasts fillets, cut into thirds
- 1 teaspoon of poultry or Italian seasoning mix
- 1 cup white cream sauce (Alfredo is fine)
- ½ cup chicken broth
- 1 cup fresh sliced mushrooms
- ½ cup diced onion
- 2 tablespoons of olive oil
- Salt and black pepper, to taste

Preparation time: 15 minutes
Cooking time: 20 minutes
Serves: 4 to 6

Directions:

1. Season the chicken with salt, pepper and poultry seasoning. In the inner pot of the pressure cooker, add the oil and press the "Meat/Chicken" button. Add the chicken and brown lightly on all sides.
2. Remove the browned chicken and set aside. Add the onions and mushrooms and cook until soft and fragrant. Press the "Keep Warm/Cancel" button.
3. Deglaze the pan using the chicken broth being sure to scrape up all the browned bits. Place the chicken back in the pot and top with the cream sauce. Stir gently.
4. Close the lid completely and slide the pressure valve to locked position.
5. Press the "Soup/Stew" button which will automatically set the pressure cooking time to 10 minutes.
6. When the pressure cooking cycle is completed, slide the pressure valve to open position to fully release the pressure. Open the lid when pressure has released. Gently stir to coat the chicken with cream sauce and adjust seasonings if desired.
7. Transfer into a serving bowl or platter and serve immediately.

CHICKEN IN BLACK BEAN SAUCE

Chicken and black bean sauce is typically thought of as a stir-fry dish, but this simple preparation is easy to prepare in your Power Pressure Cooker XL and has great flavor. Your grocery store should have jarred black bean sauce in the Asian section.

Ingredients:

- 1 pound boneless, skinless chicken breast, cubed
- 6 tablespoons of jarred black bean sauce
- 1 ½ tablespoons soy sauce
- 1 cup diced onion and pepper mixture
- 1 cup chicken broth
- 4 garlic cloves, crushed
- drizzle olive oil
- pepper, to taste
- 1 tbsp cornstarch mixed in 1 tablespoon cold water (optional for thickening)

Preparation time: 15 minutes
Cooking time: 25 minutes
Serves: 4

Directions:

1. In the inner pot of the pressure cooker, add the oil and press the "Meat/Chicken" button. Add the chicken and cook until lightly browned all sides. Stir in the peppers and onions and cook until they begin to soften. Add garlic and cook for one more minute. Press the "Keep Warm/Cancel" button.
2. Stir in the chicken broth, soy sauce and black bean sauce. Stir well to combine all ingredients.
3. Close the lid completely and slide the pressure valve to locked position.
4. Press the "Beans/Lentils" button and use the pre-programmed time of 5 minutes.
5. When the pressure cooking cycle is completed, slide the pressure valve to open position to fully release the pressure. Open the lid when pressure has released and cook further for 10 minutes in "Meat/Chicken" mode to thicken the sauce, if desired. If you desire a thick sauce, dissolve 1 tablespoon of cornstarch into 1 tablespoon of cold water. Add to the pot and simmer to thicken.
6. Gently stir to evenly coat the chicken with sauce, transfer to a serving platter bowl and serve immediately.

CHICKEN IN CHEESY SUN-DRIED TOMATO SAUCE

The chicken is juicy and succulent in this delicious, creamy sauce. I found that adding half a cup of heavy cream doesn't take away from the flavor of the pesto. If you prefer a creamier sauce, feel free to add a little more of the heavy cream. I recommend serving this over pasta. You can easily double the sauce if you like lots of sauce.

Ingredients:

- 2 pounds chicken thighs
- 1 tablespoon minced garlic
- 1 cup jarred sun-dried tomato pesto sauce
- ½ cup heavy cream
- 2 teaspoons poultry or Italian seasoning mix
- ½ cup grated Parmesan cheese
- 3 tablespoons water or broth, to thin sauce
- drizzle olive oil
- Salt and black pepper, to taste

Preparation time: 10 minutes
Cooking time: 20 minutes
Serves: 4 to 6

Directions:

1. In the inner pot of the pressure cooker, add the oil and press the "Meat/Chicken" button. Season the chicken with Italian seasoning, salt and black pepper and add into the inner pot. Cook until evenly browned on both sides, add the garlic and cook for one more minute.
2. Pour the heavy cream and the sun-dried tomato pesto into the pot. Gently stir to evenly coat the chicken with sauce and press the "Keep Warm/Cancel" button.
3. Close the lid completely and slide the pressure valve to locked position.
4. Press the "Meat/Chicken" button which will set the time to 15 minutes.
5. When the pressure cooking cycle is completed, slide the pressure valve to open position to fully release the pressure. Open the lid when pressure has released and gently stir to coat the chicken with sauce.
6. Adjust seasonings if desired. Serve immediately, topped with Parmesan cheese. This dish is excellent on its own or on top of a bed of your favorite pasta.

SPICY PEANUT CHICKEN TENDERS

Most Asian sections in the grocery store will have a jarred peanut sauce, or feel free to whip up your own. Most kids love the peanut butter flavor of the sauce with the chicken and gobble it up. Served with rice and a vegetable, this is an easy complete meal.

Ingredients:

- 1 ½ cups jarred Thai peanut or Satay sauce
- ½ cup chicken broth
- 2 pounds chicken tenders
- 1 teaspoon poultry seasoning mix
- 3 tablespoons unsalted peanuts, chopped
- Salt and black pepper, to taste
- drizzle of olive oil

Preparation time: 10 minutes
Cooking time: 20 minutes
Serves: 6 to 8

Directions:

1. In the inner pot of the pressure cooker, add the oil and press the "Meat/Chicken" button. Season the chicken with the poultry seasoning. Add the chicken tenders and cook until evenly browned on all sides while turning occasionally.
2. Stir in the remaining ingredients, except for the chopped peanuts. Season to taste with salt and pepper and press the "Keep Warm/Cancel" button.
3. Close the lid completely and slide the pressure valve to locked position.
4. Press the "Bean/Lentils" button and use the pre-programmed cooking time of 5 minutes.
5. When the pressure cooking cycle is completed, slide the pressure valve to open position to fully release the pressure. Open the lid when pressure has released and gently stir to distribute the ingredients well.
6. Adjust seasonings if desired, transfer into a serving bowl and top with chopped peanuts. Serve with rice.

CHICKEN CURRY

Our grocery store just started selling a delicious jarred Tikka Masala sauce and it so easy and so yummy! This is a perfect recipe for busy nights. Fix some rice to serve with the chicken and dinner is ready to go. If you prefer a home made sauce, instead of a pre-packaged jar that will work great, too.

Ingredients:

- 1 ½ pounds boneless, skinless chicken thighs
- 1 small onion, diced in large chunks
- ½ cup green pepper slices
- 1 cup canned, diced tomatoes
- 1 cup jarred Biryani or Tikka Masala curry sauce
- ½ cup chicken broth
- drizzle olive oil
- Salt and black pepper, to taste

Preparation time: 20 minutes
Cooking time: 25 minutes
Serves: 4-6

Directions:

1. In the inner pot of the pressure cooker, add the oil and press the "Meat/Chicken" button. Brown the chicken thighs on all sides, then set aside on a separate plate. Add onions and peppers and cook until they begin to soften.
2. Add the tomatoes, chicken broth and curry sauce and cook until it reaches to a simmer. Place the chicken back in the pot, spooning some of the sauce over the pieces. Press the "Keep Warm/Cancel" button.
3. Close the lid completely and slide the pressure valve to locked position.
4. Press the "Soup/Stew" button and use "Time Adjustment" feature to set the pressure cooking time to 12 minutes.
5. When the pressure cooking cycle is completed, slide the pressure valve to open position to fully release the pressure. Open the lid when pressure has released.
6. Adjust seasonings if desired, transfer into a serving bowl and serve immediately.

HAWAIIAN BBQ CHICKEN

This delicious meal is sure to wake up your taste buds! Sometimes a little sweet pineapple chicken in a creamy barbecue sauce is all you need to turn your day around. Serve with a small slice of lime for squeezing over the chicken.

Ingredients:

- 2 pounds of chicken tenders
- Salt and pepper, to taste
- 1 teaspoon of chili flakes or powder
- 1 cup of sweet honey BBQ Sauce
- 2 cups of canned pineapple chunks
- 1 cup low fat canned coconut milk or cream
- 2 limes, sliced into wedges for serving

Preparation time: 5 minutes
Cooking time: 20 minutes
Serves: 6

Directions:

1. In the inner pot, combine together the pineapple, BBQ sauce, coconut cream, and chili flakes. Season the chicken with salt and pepper and add to the sauce. Toss to evenly coat with the sauce mixture.
2. Close the lid completely and slide pressure valve to locked position.
3. Press the "Beans/Lentils" button and use pre-programmed cooking time of 5 minutes.
4. When the pressure cooking cycle is completed, slide the pressure valve to open position to fully release the pressure. Open the lid when pressure has released. Remove the chicken with a pair of tongs and cook the sauce further in "Meat/Chicken" mode until it has thickened, if desired.
5. Return the chicken and gently toss to evenly coat with the sauce mixture.
6. Transfer to serving bowl or platter and serve immediately, with sliced lime for flavor and garnish.

HONEY MUSTARD CHICKEN

Our family loves honey mustard, so this is a favorite in our house. By using a mallet to pound the chicken to equal thickness, you will insure that the chicken is cooked equally and stays juicy. Try to marinade for at least a few hours, it adds so much flavor to the dish. To crisp up the top, try broiling it for a few minutes after it is cooked

Ingredients:

- 4 medium sized chicken breasts
- ¼ cup dijon mustard
- ½ cup honey
- 2 teaspoons chopped garlic
- ½ teaspoon paprika
- ½ cup chicken broth
- drizzle olive oil
- salt and pepper, to taste

Preparation time: 5 minutes
Cooking time: 20 minutes
Serves: 4

Directions:

1. Mix together mustard, honey, broth and paprika. Use a mallet to pound the chicken breast so they are all of equal thickness. Marinate the chicken breasts in the honey mustard mixture for a few hours or overnight.
2. In the inner pot of the pressure cooker, add the oil and press the "Meat/Chicken" button. Add the garlic and sauté until soft and fragrant. Pour the chicken and sauce mixture into the pot and press the "Keep Warm/ Cancel" button.
3. Close the lid completely and slide the pressure valve to locked position.
4. Press the "Beans/Lentils" button use "Time Adjustment" button to adjust pressure cooking time to 8 minutes.
5. When the pressure cooking cycle is completed, slide the pressure valve to open position to fully release the pressure. Open the lid when pressure has released and gently stir to coat the chicken with sauce. Adjust seasoning if desired.
6. Transfer into a serving bowl and serve immediately.

CHICKEN AND DUMPLINGS

Easy and super, simple comfort food at its finest! Using the refrigerated biscuits is not only very easy, but makes for very tasty dumplings. If you don't like to use creamed soups, use your favorite homemade preparation. I like to use carrot and onion in our chicken and dumplings, but use whatever you have on hand and taylor it to your family's taste.

Ingredients:

- 4 boneless, skinless chicken breasts, cut in pieces
- 2 cups chopped vegetables of choice (carrots, onions, potatoes and peas are good ideas)
- 1 can cream of chicken soup
- 3 tablespoons butter
- 1 can refrigerated biscuit dough (not the jumbo variety) cut into quarters
- 3 cups chicken broth
- salt and pepper, to taste

Preparation time: 10 minutes
Cooking time: 40 minutes
Serves: 4 to 6

Directions:

1. In the inner pot of the pressure cooker, add the butter and press the "Meat/Chicken" button. Cook the vegetables while the butter melts. Add the chicken and season with salt and pepper.
2. Stir in the cream of chicken soup and the broth. Mix ingredients well. Add the quartered biscuit dough to the top and season to taste. Press the "Keep Warm/Cancel" button.
3. Close the lid completely and slide the pressure valve to locked position.
4. Press the "Beans/Lentils" button and use pre-programmed cook time of 5 minutes.
5. When the pressure cooking cycle is completed, allow the pressure to release naturally. Open the lid when pressure has released.
6. Briefly stir to evenly distribute the ingredients, transfer into a serving bowl and serve immediately.

ASIAN STYLE BARBECUE CHICKEN

You should be able to find Asian barbecue sauce in the Asian section of your grocery store. Just a simple spice rub to the chicken and a few additions to the sauce, like the garlic and the brown sugar, make this a recipe you will want to prepare again and again!

Ingredients:

- 2 pounds chicken thighs, bone-in
- 1 cup jarred Asian barbecue sauce
- 1 teaspoon BBQ spice-rub mix
- 3 garlic cloves, chopped
- 1 tablespoon of brown sugar
- ¼ cup water
- drizzle olive oil
- 3 tablespoons chopped green onion (optional, for serving)

Preparation time: 15 minutes
Cooking time: 25 minutes
Serves: 4 to 6

Directions:

1. Rub the chicken with the spice mix evenly on all sides and set aside.
2. In the inner pot of the pressure cooker, add the oil and press the "Meat/Chicken" button. Add the chicken and cook until the meat is evenly browned on both sides. Add the garlic and cook for another 1-2 minutes.
3. Add in the barbecue sauce, water and brown sugar, stir to combine and press the "Keep Warm/Cancel" button.
4. Close the lid completely and slide the pressure valve to locked position.
5. Press the "Meat/Chicken" button and use the pre-programmed cooking time of 15 minutes.
6. When the pressure cooking cycle is completed, slide the pressure valve to open position to fully release the pressure. Open the lid when pressure has released.
7. Stir to coat the chicken evenly with the sauce. Remove the chicken with a pair of tongs and cook the sauce in "Meat/Chicken" mode until it has thickened, stirring regularly. When sauce has reached desired consistency, pour it over the chicken thighs and top with green onions.

WHOLE ROAST CHICKEN

The medley of seasonings add perfect flavor to this chicken and the lemon adds a nice, light undertone. The bottom of the chicken will cook in the liquid, so if you prefer your chicken to be out of the liquid, place it on the steamer tray after it has been browned.

Ingredients:

- 4 pound whole chicken
- 1 teaspoon paprika
- 1 ½ teaspoons poultry seasoning mix
- 2 tablespoons lemon juice
- 6 cloves peeled garlic
- 1 ½ cups chicken broth
- Salt and black pepper, to taste
- drizzle olive oil

Preparation time: 10 minutes
Cooking time: 50 minutes
Serves: 4-6

Directions:

1. Season the chicken breast fillets with paprika, poultry seasoning, salt and pepper and set aside.
2. In the inner pot of the pressure cooker, add the oil and press the "Meat/Chicken" button. Brown the chicken with the breast side down for about 6 minutes. Flip the chicken over and pour in the lemon juice and broth. Throw the garlic in the bottom of the pot. Press the "Keep Warm/Cancel" button.
3. Close the lid completely and slide the pressure valve to locked position.
4. Press the "Rice/Risotto" button and use "Cook Time Selector" button twice to set the pressure cooking time to 25 minutes.
5. When the pressure cooking cycle is completed, allow the pressure to release naturally. Open the lid when pressure has released.
6. Remove the chicken from the pot and allow to rest for 5 minutes before serving.

CHICKEN ALFREDO

Classic chicken Alfredo, cooked in no time at all in the Power Pressure Cooker XL! If only all dinners were this tasty and easy. If you don't like to use jarred Alfredo sauce, your homemade version will be wonderful, too. When you add the noodles to the pot, make sure they are covered in liquid before sealing the pot. Add more broth or water if necessary.

Ingredients:

- 2 large chicken breasts, cut into cubes
- 2 jars Alfredo sauce
- 1 box Linguine pasta
- 1 cup chicken broth
- 1 cup sliced mushrooms (optional)
- 1-2 tablespoons minced garlic
- drizzle olive oil
- Salt and black pepper, to taste

Preparation time: 15 minutes
Cooking time: 15 minutes
Serves: 6 to 8

Directions:

1. Season the chicken with salt and pepper and set aside.
2. In the inner pot of the pressure cooker, add the oil and press the "Meat/Chicken" button. Add the chicken, cook until starting to brown on both sides and stir in the mushrooms if you choose to use them. Cook for about 3 minutes. Add garlic and cook for one more minute. Stir to combine and press the "Keep Warm/Cancel" button.
3. Break the dry pasta in half and add to the bottom of the pot. Use a spatula or spoon to move most of the chicken-mushroom mixture on top of the pasta. Pour in the two jars of Alfredo sauce and the chicken broth.
4. Close the lid completely and slide the pressure valve to locked position.
5. Press the "Beans/Lentils" button and use pre-programmed cook time of 5 minutes.
6. When the pressure cooking cycle is completed, slide the pressure valve to open position to fully release the pressure. Open the lid when pressure has released.
7. Adjust seasonings if desired, transfer into a serving bowl and serve immediately.

CHICKEN IN LEMON GARLIC SAUCE

Chicken thighs are delicious, with their dark meat that stays tender and juicy. This lemon, garlic sauce is a succulent ,but light flavor that compliments the chicken so well.

Ingredients:

- 2 pounds chicken thighs
- 2 teaspoons poultry seasoning
- 1 large lemon, juiced
- ¼ cup white wine
- ½ cup chicken broth
- 5 cloves garlic, minced
- salt and pepper, to taste
- drizzle oil
- 1 tablespoon cornstarch (optional for thickening the sauce)

Preparation time: 10 minutes
Cooking time: 20 minutes
Serves: 4 to 6

Directions:

1. Season chicken thighs with poultry seasoning, salt and pepper and set aside.
2. In the inner pot of the pressure cooker, add the oil and press the "Meat/Chicken" button. Add the chicken and cook until it is evenly browned on all sides. Add the garlic and cook for 1 minute. Stir in the remaining ingredients, stir to combine and press the "Keep Warm/Cancel" button.
3. Close the lid completely and slide the pressure valve to locked position.
4. Press the "Soup/Stew" button and use "Time Adjustment" feature to set the pressure cooking time to 12 minutes.
5. When the pressure cooking cycle is completed, slide the pressure valve to open position to fully release the pressure. Open the lid when pressure has released.
6. Adjust seasonings if desired and gently stir to evenly coat the chicken with sauce. If you are using cornstarch to thicken the sauce, dissolve the cornstarch into 2 tablespoons cold water. Pour this mixture into the pot and press the "Meat/Chicken" button. Stir well until sauce begins to simmer and reaches desired consistency. Transfer to a serving platter and serve immediately.

CHEESY STUFFED CHICKEN IN ALFREDO SAUCE

My kids and I love this recipe! The chicken is always cooked just right and the Alfredo sauce makes a delicious topping, not only for the chicken, but also for the green vegetables we always serve on the side. The recipe is easy to put together and has dinner on the table in no time at all.

Ingredients:

- 4 chicken breast fillets, pounded thin
- ¾ to 1 cup packaged, shredded three cheese (Monterey jack, Colby, Cheddar cheese)
- 1 ½ cups Alfredo sauce
- Salt and pepper, to taste
- 1 teaspoon of mixed Italian herbs or poultry seasoning mix
- drizzle oil

Preparation time: 15 minutes
Cooking time: 20 minutes
Serves: 4

Directions:

1. Season the flattened breast fillet with Italian herbs/poultry seasoning, salt and pepper. Place about 3 to 4 tablespoons of shredded cheese on top of each chicken piece and roll it upwards. Secure each roll with a toothpick and set aside.
2. In the inner pot of the pressure cooker, add the oil and press the "Meat/Chicken" button. Brown the stuffed chicken breast evenly on both sides and pour in the Alfredo sauce. Press the "Keep Warm/Cancel" button.
3. Close the lid completely and slide the pressure valve to locked position.
4. Press the "Soup/Stew" button and use pre-programed cooking time of 10 minutes.
5. When the pressure cooking cycle is completed, slide the pressure valve to open position to fully release the pressure. Open the lid when pressure has released.
6. Adjust seasonings if desired and transfer to a serving platter or bowl. Top with leftover cheese and serve immediately.

CHICKEN MARSALA

Easy, simple and classic, this Chicken Marsala recipe will be used over and over in your house.

Ingredients:

- 1 ½ pounds boneless, skinless chicken thighs
- 2 cups sliced mushrooms
- 1 cup Marsala wine
- 2 cloves garlic, minced
- ½ cup chicken broth
- ¼ cup cornstarch
- Salt and black pepper, to taste
- drizzle oil
- Chopped parsley (optional, for serving)

Preparation time: **10** *minutes*
Cooking time: **20** *minutes*
Serves: **4**

Directions:

1. Season the chicken liberally with salt and pepper. Add the oil to the inner pot and press the "Meat/Chicken" button. Add the chicken and brown lightly on both sides. In the last two minutes, add the garlic. Press the "Keep Warm/Cancel" button.
2. Pour in the Marsala wine and add the mushrooms. Close the lid completely and slide the pressure valve to locked position.
3. Press the "Soup/Stew" button and use the pre-programmed cooking time of 10 minutes.
4. When the pressure cooking cycle is completed, slide the pressure valve to open position to fully release the pressure. Open the lid when pressure has released.
5. Transfer the chicken pieces to a platter. Press the "Meat/Chicken" button to bring remaining liquid to a boil.
6. In a separate bowl, mix together the chicken stock and corn starch until there are no lumps. Pour into the pot and stir gently until sauce reaches desired thickness. Add the chicken back to the pot. Press the "Keep Warm/Cancel" button.
7. Serve the chicken and sauce over egg noddles with chopped parsley on top as a garnish.

HONEY GLAZED CHICKEN TENDERS

This is sure to delight all the kiddos in your life, and the adults, too. This recipe tastes a bit like Chinese take-out and is wonderful with a side of rice.

Ingredients:

- 2 pounds chicken tenders, (boneless, skinless)
- ½ cup honey
- ¼ cup light soy sauce
- ½ cup tomato ketchup
- 2 teaspoons of minced garlic
- 1 tablespoon cornstarch
- 2 tablespoons water
- ½ teaspoon freshly ground black pepper, more to taste

Preparation time: 5 minutes
Cooking time: 20 minutes
Serves: 6

Directions:

1. In the inner pot of the pressure cooker, mix together all ingredients except for the chicken, water and cornstarch and stir to combine. Add the chicken and gently toss to coat evenly with the sauce mixture.
2. Close the lid completely and slide the pressure valve to locked position.
3. Press the "Rice/Risotto" button and use the pre-programmed time of 6 minutes.
4. While the chicken is cooking, dissolve 1 tablespoon of cornstarch into 2 tablespoons of cold water.
5. When the pressure cooking cycle is completed, slide the pressure valve to open position to fully release the pressure. Open the lid when pressure has released.
6. Gently stir to evenly coat the chicken with honey garlic sauce. Add the cornstarch mixture to the sauce and press the "Meat/Chicken" button. Cook , stirring frequently, until sauce begins to simmer and thickens to desired consistency.
7. Transfer to a serving platter or bowl and serve immediately.

BRAISED CHICKEN IN MOLE SAUCE

The mole sauce is the star of the show here, so find your favorite, whether it is jarred or homemade. Traditional mole sauce is a Mexican staple made from tomatoes, chilies and dark chocolate. Enjoy this simple take using the Power Pressure Cooker XL for perfect juicy chicken in this classic sauce.

Ingredients:

- 8 chicken thighs
- 1 cup jarred mole sauce
- 1 cup chicken broth (low sodium)
- 1 teaspoon poultry seasoning
- 3 tablespoons lime juice
- 1 teaspoon toasted sesame seeds
- drizzle olive oil

Preparation time: 15 minutes
Cooking time: 20 minutes
Serves: 6 to 8

Directions:

1. In the inner pot of the pressure cooker, add the oil and press the "Meat/Chicken" button. Add the chicken, season with poultry seasoning and brown evenly on all sides.
2. Add the lime juice to the pot and use it to deglaze the bottom. Scrape at the browned bits. Press the "Keep Warm/Cancel" button.
3. In a separate bowl, combine together the mole sauce and chicken broth and stir until well combined. Pour the sauce over the chicken thighs.
4. Close the lid completely and slide the pressure valve to locked position.
5. Press the "Soup/Stew" button and use "Time Adjustment" feature to set the pressure cooking time to 12 minutes.
6. When the pressure cooking cycle is completed, slide the pressure valve to open position to fully release the pressure. Open the lid when pressure has released.
7. Transfer chicken and sauce to a serving platter or bowl, top with toasted sesame seeds and serve immediately.

APRICOT-ORANGE CHICKEN BREAST

This is a fruity chicken preparation with great seasoning provided by the onion soup mix. This recipe is very easy to prepare and will be enjoyed by both children and adults.

Ingredients:

- 4 boneless, skinless chicken breasts, pounded to even thickness
- ½ cup apricot preserve
- ½ cup orange marmalade
- 1 cup chicken broth
- 1 envelope onion soup mix
- drizzle olive oil

Preparation time: 10 minutes
Cooking time: 20 minutes
Serves: 4

Directions:

1. In the inner pot of the pressure cooker, add the oil and press the "Meat/Chicken" button. Add the chicken and brown evenly on both sides.
2. Combine together all ingredients in a bowl and mix to combine. Pour mixture into the inner pot and gently stir to evenly coat the chicken with the sauce mixture. Press the "Keep Warm/Cancel" button.
3. Close the lid completely and slide the pressure valve to locked position.
4. Press the "Soup/Stew" button and use the pre-programmed time of 10 minutes.
5. When the pressure cooking cycle is completed, slide the pressure valve to open position to fully release the pressure. Open the lid when pressure has released. Remove the chicken and cook further to thicken the sauce, if desired, by using the "Meat/Chicken" feature.
6. Transfer the chicken to a serving platter or bowl, pour the sauce over the chicken and serve immediately.

MEXI-CALI CHICKEN

This is a favorite in our household and has so may possibilities. The chicken is more sweet than spicy, so even the kids love it. Serve it over a salad or on a burrito with plenty of avocado and chips and salsa.

Ingredients:

- 4 chicken breast,
- ½ cup salsa
- 1 tablespoon cumin
- ½ cup brown sugar
- 1 (4 ounce) can diced green chilies
- 6 ounces Sprite (½ can)

Preparation time: **5** *minutes*
Cooking time: **20** *minutes*
Serves: **4**

Directions:

1. In the inner pot of the pressure cooker, mix together all ingredients except for the chicken.
2. Add the chicken to the pot and use a spoon to pour the sauce mixture over the top of the breasts.
3. Close the lid completely and slide the pressure valve to locked position.
4. Press the "Soup/Stew" button and use the pre-programmed time of 10 minutes.
5. When the pressure cooking cycle is completed, slide the pressure valve to open position to fully release the pressure. Open the lid when pressure has released.
6. Remove the chicken and shred with a fork. Put back into the pot and mix with the sauce. Serve immediately. This recipe is great as protein for a salad or burrito and is also good with rice.

CAJUN CHICKEN

This is a hearty, wholesome meal that has plenty of flavor and just enough spicy kick. You can make it spicier by using a can of Rotel and add more of the Cajun seasoning or perhaps a sprinkle of cayenne pepper. Serve over a bed of rice for a simple, but delicious dinner.

Ingredients:

- 8 bone-in chicken thighs
- 3 tablespoons Cajun seasoning, divided
- 2 cups frozen chopped onion and pepper
- 1 can diced tomatoes or Rotel, for added heat
- 1 can red beans, rinsed and drained
- 1 cup chicken broth
- drizzle olive oil

Preparation time: 10 minutes
Cooking time: 20 minutes
Serves: 6

Directions:

1. In the inner pot of the pressure cooker, add the oil and press the "Meat/Chicken" button. Season the chicken with 1 tablespoon of Cajun seasoning. Add the chicken to the pot and brown lightly on both sides.
2. Mix together all ingredients except for the chicken and stir to combine. Pour on top of the chicken and gently toss to evenly coat with the sauce mixture. Press the "Keep Warm/Cancel" button.
3. Close the lid completely and slide the pressure valve to locked position.
4. Press the "Soup/Stew" button and use "Time Adjustment" feature to set the pressure cooking time to 12 minutes.
5. When the pressure cooking cycle is completed, slide the pressure valve to open position to fully release the pressure. Open the lid when pressure has released.
6. Adjust seasonings if desired, and serve the chicken and tomato pepper mixture over a bed of rice.

PINEAPPLE SALSA CHICKEN

This flavorful, fruity chicken dish is a snap to prepare. Use jarred or homemade salsa, whatever you prefer. Both pineapple and mango are both delicious, so I suggest you try both and pick your favorite!

Ingredients:

- 2 pounds boneless, skinless chicken breast, cut into thirds
- 2 cups pineapple or mango salsa
- ½ cup of chicken broth
- 1 teaspoon minced garlic
- salt and pepper, to taste
- 2 tablespoons of olive or cooking oil

Preparation time: 10 minutes
Cooking time: 20 minutes
Serves: 4 to6

Directions:

1. In the inner pot of the pressure cooker, add the oil and press the "Meat/Chicken" button. Add the chicken and cook until lightly browned. Add the garlic and cook for one more minute.
2. Press the "Keep Warm/Cancel" button and stir in the remaining ingredients.
3. Close the lid completely and slide the pressure valve to locked position.
4. Press the "Rice/Risotto" button which will automatically set the pressure cooking time to 6 minutes.
5. When the pressure cooking cycle is completed, slide the pressure valve to open position to fully release the pressure. Open the lid when pressure has released.
6. Gently toss to coat the chicken with the sauce, transfer to a serving platter or bowl and serve immediately.

ROSEMARY LEMON CHICKEN

This is an easy and tasty way to prepare a whole chicken that will be juicy and flavorful. Browning the chicken before cooking will add some color and flavor to the skin, just like a traditional roast chicken! It can be a bit cumbersome to flip, so try using tongs, spatula or both. If you don't have fresh rosemary (which I highly recommend) dried rosemary will work just fine. Sprinkle on the outside of the bird and inside the cavity for added flavor.

Ingredients:

- 4 pound whole chicken
- Salt and black pepper, to taste
- 1 cup of chicken broth
- 4 lemons, sliced into halves, plus the zest from one of those lemons
- 1 head of garlic, cloves divided
- 4 sprigs of fresh rosemary
- 2 tablespoons olive oil

Preparation time: 15 minutes
Cooking time: 60 minutes
Serves: 4 to 6

Directions:

1. Wash your chicken and pat it dry.
2. Chop one of the springs of fresh rosemary to make about 1 tablespoon of chopped rosemary. In a small bowl, combine together the lemon zest, 1 tablespoon of rosemary, 1 ½ tablespoons olive oil, 4 cloves of garlic (mashed) and salt and pepper to taste. Rub this mixture all over the bird, including under the wings and legs. Place 2 halves of lemon and the remaining sprigs of rosemary into the cavity of the chicken.
3. Using the "Meat/Chicken" button, add a drizzle of live oil to the inner pot and brown the chicken, breast side down, for about 4 minutes. Flip the chicken to brown the other side and remove the chicken when down.
4. In the inner pot of the pressure cooker, pour in the stock and use it to deglaze the pan. Scrape at the browned bits on the bottom of the pan. Arrange the lemon halves and garlic in the bottom of the pot and place the chicken on top. Press the "Keep Warm/Cancel" button.
5. Close the lid completely and slide the pressure valve to locked position.
6. Press the "Rice/Risotto" button and press "Cook Time Selector" button twice to set the pressure cooking time to 25 minutes.
7. When the pressure cooking cycle is completed, allow the pressure to release naturally. Open the lid when pressure has released. Remove the chicken, transfer to a plate and set aside. Remove and discard the lemons, rosemary and garlic and season the chicken if desired.
8. Transfer the chicken to a serving platter and serve immediately.

ORANGE CRANBERRY TURKEY BREAST

Now you can have Thanksgiving style turkey any time your desire! With turkey breast, it can be easy to wind up with a dry, flavorless bird. That's not the case with the Power Pressure Cooker XL! I think you'll find this to be full of flavor and very juicy. The sauce makes for a delicious, sweet gravy to serve with the meat.

Ingredients:

- 4 pound boneless turkey breast
- 3 cups orange juice
- 1 packet onion soup mix
- 1 can whole cranberry sauce
- 2 tablespoons cornstarch
- salt and pepper, to taste
- drizzle olive oil

Preparation time: 10 minutes
Cooking time: 60 minutes
Serves: 4 to 6

Directions:

1. In the inner pot of the pressure cooker, add the oil and press the "Meat/Chicken" button. Season the turkey breast and place it in the pot to brown lightly on all sides. Remove when finished and set on a plate.
2. In the pot, whisk together the remaining ingredients. Place the turkey breast, skin side down and use a spoon to coat the breast in the sauce. Press the "Keep Warm/Cancel" button.
3. Close the lid completely and slide the pressure valve to locked position.
4. Press the "Beans/Lentils" button and push the "Cook Time Selector" button twice to set the pressure cooking time to 30 minutes.
5. When the pressure cooking cycle is completed, allow the pressure to release naturally. Open the lid when pressure has released. Remove the turkey, transfer to a plate and set aside.
6. If you wish to make a gravy from the sauce, remove about ½ cup of the sauce from the pot. Dissolve 2 tablespoons of cornstarch until there are no lumps. Add the mixture back to the pot and press the "Meat/Chicken" button. Stir frequently until sauce reaches desired consistency.
7. Carve and serve immediately with the warm gravy over top.

Pork

PORK AFRITADA

This is a traditional Fillipino dish, that is essentially pork stewed in tomato sauce. By adapting this recipe to the Power Pressure Cooker XL, you are able to achieve the flavors associated with stewed pork without the hassle of standing over the stove. Feel free to add a little carrot or potato to the dish to add even more sustenance and flavor.

Ingredients:

- 1 ½ pounds of pork belly, cut into cubes
- 2 cups jarred tomato basil garlic sauce
- 1 cup diced red onion
- 1 cup diced red and green bell pepper
- 1 cup chicken or vegetable broth
- 3 bay leaves
- Salt and black pepper, to taste
- drizzle olive oil

Preparation time: 10 minutes
Cooking time: 30 minutes
Serves: 4

Directions:

1. In the inner pot of the pressure cooker, press the "Meat/Chicken" button and add the oil and the pork. Season to taste with salt and pepper and cook until evenly browned on all sides. Stir in the onions and sweet pepper and cook until the vegetables are soft and fragrant. Stir in the rest of the ingredients and press the "Keep Warm/Cancel" button.
2. Close the lid completely and slide the pressure valve to locked position.
3. Press the "Meat/Chicken" button and use the "Time Adjustment" feature to set the pressure cooking time to 20 minutes.
4. When the pressure cooking cycle is completed, slide the pressure valve to open position to fully release the pressure. Open the lid when pressure has released.
5. Adjust seasonings if desired, transfer into a serving bowl and serve immediately.

APRICOT GLAZED PORK TENDERLOIN

This apricot glaze is a surprising sauce that is both sweet (from the apricots) and zesty (from the mustard). Both are a perfect pairing for the pork. Even the kids at the table enjoy this dish!

Ingredients:

- 2 pounds pork tenderloin, sliced into several large pieces
- 1 ½ cups apricot preserves
- 2 tablespoons spicy brown mustard
- 2 teaspoons minced garlic
- 1 cup chicken stock
- ¼ teaspoon dried thyme
- Salt and black pepper, to taste
- drizzle olive oil

Preparation time: 10 minutes
Cooking time: 35 minutes
Serves: 4 to 6

Directions:

1. Season the pork with salt and pepper and set aside.
2. In the inner pot of the pressure cooker, add the oil and press the "Meat/Chicken" button. Add the pork and sear until lightly browned on all sides. Add the garlic and cook for one minute.
3. Whisk together the remaining ingredients and pour into the inner pot. Press the "Keep Warm/Cancel" button.
4. Close the lid completely and slide the pressure valve to locked position.
5. Press the "Meat/Chicken" button and use the "Time Adjustment" feature to set the pressure cooking time to 20 minutes.
6. When the pressure cooking cycle is completed, slide the pressure valve to open position to fully release the pressure. Open the lid when pressure has released.
7. Adjust seasonings if desired, transfer to a serving plate and serve immediately, topped with the apricot sauce.

PORK CHOPS WITH MUSHROOM GRAVY

Pork chops and gravy are ultimate comfort food. The pork chops are tender and juicy and coated in a thick gravy designed to stick to your ribs. Serve this on a cold winter night with some buttery mashed potatoes and a side salad.

Ingredients:

- 4 pork chops, bone-in
- 1 cup button mushroom
- 1 small onion, sliced into rounds
- 1 can cream of mushroom soup
- 1 ½ cups chicken broth
- 2 tablespoons corn starch dissolved in 2 tablespoons cold water
- Salt and black pepper, to taste
- drizzle olive oil

Directions:

1. Season the pork chops with salt and pepper and set aside.
2. In the inner pot of the pressure cooker, add the oil and press the "Meat/Chicken" button. Add the pork chops and cook until evenly browned on both sides. Remove from pot. Stir in the onions and mushrooms and cook for about 3-5 minutes, or until soft and fragrant. Add the pork chops back to the pot.
3. Pour in the chicken broth and mushroom soup and press the "Keep Warm/Cancel" button.
4. Close the lid completely and slide the pressure valve to locked position.
5. Press the "Meat/Chicken" button and use the "Time Adjustment" feature to set the pressure cooking time to 18 minutes.
6. When the pressure cooking cycle is completed, slide the pressure valve to open position to fully release the pressure. Open the lid when pressure has released.
7. Remove the pork chops and place on a plate. Dissolve 2 tablespoons corn starch into 2 tablespoons cold water and stir into the pot to thicken the gravy if desired. Press the "Meat/Chicken" button and simmer until desired thickness is reached.
8. Adjust seasonings if desired, pour the gravy over the chops and serve immediately.

Preparation time: 10 minutes
Cooking time: 35 minutes
Serves: 4

PLUM SAUCED PORK RIBS

Check out the Asian section of your grocery store to find bottled plum sauce to prepare this delicious rib recipe. Plum sauce is a tangy, sweet and sour sauce that you will love as a rib coating and dipping sauce.

Ingredients:

- 2 pounds pork ribs
- 1 ¼ cups canned/bottled plum sauce
- 2 tablespoons apple cider vinegar
- 1 cup diced white onion
- 1 teaspoon mixed herbs
- 1 cup dried plums
- ¼ cup water
- Salt and black pepper, to taste
- drizzle olive oil

Preparation time: 15 minutes
Cooking time: 5 minutes
Serves: 4 to 6

Directions:

1. Season the pork with salt and pepper, rub evenly on all areas and set aside.
2. In the inner pot of the pressure cooker, add 1 tablespoon of oil and press the "Meat/Chicken" button. Place the pork ribs in the pot and cook until evenly browned on all sides. Remove the ribs and brown the onions until soft and fragrant.
3. Mix in the rest of the ingredients including the ribs, stir to combine and press the "Keep Warm/Cancel" button.
4. Press the "Meat/Chicken" button and use the "Time Adjustment" feature to set the pressure cooking time to 20 minutes.
5. When the pressure cooking cycle is completed, allow the pressure to release naturally. Slide the pressure valve to open position to fully release the pressure. Open the lid when pressure has released.
6. Adjust seasonings if needed. Transfer ribs and plums to a serving platter. Serve with the extra sauce if desired.

CHIPOTLE PORK LOIN

Pork loin was made for the Power Pressure Cooker XL. The pork loin can sometimes turn into a tough, dry cut of meat if not cooked properly, but that's never a worry with the Power Pressure Cooker XL. This marinade adds just a little kick to flavor up your meal and the meat will be tender and delicious.

Ingredients:

- 2 ½ pound pork loin, trimmed of excess fat
- ¾ cup orange juice, divided
- 2 tablespoons dark brown sugar
- 2 chipotle chili peppers in adobo (canned variety) plus 1 tablespoon of the sauce
- 1 tablespoon garlic, minced
- 3 tablespoons olive oil, divided
- 1 teaspoon salt, plus salt and pepper, to taste

Preparation time: 15 minutes
Cooking time:
1 hour, 15 minutes
Serves: 6

Directions:

1. Combine together ¼ cup orange juice, 2 tablespoons olive oil, brown sugar, chipotle peppers and 1 tablespoon sauce, garlic and 1 teaspoon salt. Pulse in a blender or food processor until completely smooth. Place liquid in a large plastic ziplock bag and add the pork. Marinade in the refrigerator overnight.
2. When ready to cook the pork, add 1 tablespoon olive oil to the inner pot and press the "Meat/Chicken" button. Remove pork from the marinade, reserving the marinade. Season the pork lightly and add to the inner pot. Brown lightly on all sides. Add the marinade to the pot along with the remaining ½ cup orange juice. Stir lightly.
3. Close the lid completely and slide the pressure valve to locked position.
4. Press the "Meat/Chicken" button and set the pressure cooking time to 25 minutes.
5. When the pressure cooking cycle is completed,allow the pressure to release naturally. Open the lid when pressure has released.
6. Adjust seasonings if desired, transfer into a serving bowl or platter and serve immediately with the sauce over the top.

SAUSAGE AND PEPPERS

This classic dish is so simple to create with the Power Pressure Cooker XL doing all the work of making sure the onions and peppers are soft and flavorful in a delicious tomato broth. I like to use large chunks of fresh bell peppers and onions, but the store packages pre-chopped frozen ones work great, too!

Ingredients:

- 1 package sweet Italian sausage links (about 2 pounds)
- 1 (28 ounce) can crushed tomatoes
- 1 (15 ounce) can tomato sauce
- 1 ½ tablespoons Italian Seasoning
- 1 teaspoon garlic, minced
- 2-3 cups chopped onion and bell pepper
- salt and pepper, to taste
- drizzle olive oil

Preparation time: 15 minutes
Cooking time: 40 minutes
Serves: 4-6

Directions:

1. In the inner pot of the pressure cooker, add the oil and press the "Meat/Chicken" button. Begin by sautéing the garlic until soft and fragrant. Add the sausage links and brown lightly. Stir in the remaining ingredients and press the "Keep Warm/Cancel" button.
2. Close the lid completely and slide the pressure valve to locked position.
3. Press the "Rice/Risotto" button and then press the "Cook Time Selector" button twice to and set the pressure cooking time to 25 minutes.
4. When the pressure cooking cycle is completed, slide the pressure valve to open position to fully release the pressure. Open the lid when pressure has released.
5. Stir gently to mix the flavors and serve immediately.

PORK IN SWEET BLACK BEAN SAUCE

This recipe requires little prep, making it a super choice for busy nights. The honey, soy sauce and pineapple create a sauce that usually tempts even the pickiest of eaters. Serve it up with some rice and a green vegetable for an easy, complete meal.

Ingredients:

- 2 pounds pork tenderloin cut into chunks
- ½ cup honey
- ¼ soy sauce
- 3 tablespoons canned Chinese black bean sauce
- 3 bay leaves
- ½ cup pineapple juice
- 1 cup mixed diced sweet peppers and onions (optional)

> Preparation time: 10 minutes
> Cooking time: 40 minutes
> Serves: 4 to 6

Directions:

1. In the inner pot of the pressure cooker, mix together all ingredients and stir to combine. Press the "Keep Warm/Cancel" button.
2. Close the lid completely and slide the pressure valve to locked position.
3. Press the "Soup/Stew" button and use the pre-programmed time of 10 minutes.
4. When the pressure cooking cycle is completed, slide the pressure valve to open position to fully release the pressure. Open the lid when pressure has released.
5. Stir to evenly coat the pork with the sauce, transfer into a serving bowl or platter and serve immediately.

KALUA PORK

Traditional kalua pork is cooked in a giant underground pit called an imu. Preparing the pit and cooking the meat can take all day, which is not a luxury most of us have! But this Power Pressure Cooker XL kalua pork is the next best this to being at a Hawaiian luau. Just a few ingredients are required to make this dish, so be sure to use actual Hawaiian sea salt for the best flavor.

Ingredients:

- 3 pounds of pork butt or shoulder roast
- 2 teaspoons of Hawaiian sea salt
- 1 tablespoon liquid smoke flavoring
- 3 tablespoons of olive oil
- 1 cup chicken stock

Preparation time: 10 minutes
Cooking time: 2 hours
Serves: 10 to 12

Directions:

1. Season the pork with the liquid smoke and the Hawaiian salt on all sides and set aside.
2. In the inner pot of the pressure cooker, add the oil and press the "Meat/Chicken" button. Place the pork and cook until evenly seared on all sides. Pour the chicken stock into the pot. Press the "Keep Warm/Cancel" button.
3. Close the lid completely and slide the pressure valve to locked position.
4. Press the "Canning/Preserving" button and set the pressure cooking time to 90 minutes.
5. When the pressure cooking cycle is completed, allow the pressure to release naturally. Open the lid when pressure has released.
6. Remove the pork and shred with a fork. Place the pork back into the pot to absorb the cooking liquid. Serve immediately. This pork is great on its own, but is also delicious over a salad or on a bun.

GLAZED HONEY HAM

This is the perfect holiday meal because it doesn't require hours of prep and cooking time. The chef still has plenty of time to prepare other items or visit with friends and family, because that's what the holidays are truly about! This recipe will deliver a perfectly sweetened, savory ham in no time at all.

Ingredients:

- 6-7 pound ham, boneless
- ½ cup honey
- 1 cup brown sugar
- 1 teaspoon ground cloves
- 4 tablespoons crushed pineapple, juice included
- 1 cup water

Preparation time: 5 minutes
Cooking time: 25 minutes
Serves: 8 to 10

Directions:

1. Prepare the ham by slicing it as you would for serving. This will help distribute the glaze.
2. In the inner pot of the pressure cooker, add 1 cup of water and the steamer tray. Create a sling using tin foil to help remove the ham when it is done cooking.
3. Place the sliced ham in a tinfoil packet. Sprinkle with brown sugar and drizzle with the honey. Distribute the cloves evenly and top with the pineapple and juice. Close the packet and place on the steam rack.
4. Close the lid completely and slide the pressure valve to locked position.
5. Press the "Soup/Stew" setting and use the pre-programmed time of 10 minutes.
6. When the pressure cooking cycle is completed, slide the pressure valve to open position to fully release the pressure. Open the lid when pressure has released.
7. Transfer the ham to a serving platter and serve immediately with the sauce in a separate serving sauce bowl.

HICKORY SMOKED BARBECUE PORK RIBS

By taking just a few minutes to prepare these ribs with a dry rub, you will elevate them from pretty good to delicious! If you have a little paprika in your cabinet, add this to your dry rub as it will enhance the smoky flavor. If the sauce is too thin for your liking, use the "Meat/Chicken" button to boil until it thickens a little.

Ingredients:

- 2 pounds pork ribs, cut into 4 portions
- 1 ½ cups hickory smoked barbecue sauce
- 3 tablespoons of BBQ dry rub
- ½ cup brown sugar
- ¾ to 1 cup chicken stock
- 2 tablespoons apple cider vinegar
- drizzle olive oil

Preparation time: 5 minutes
Cooking time: 50 minutes
Serves: 4

Directions:

1. Season the pork with BBQ dry rub on all sides and set aside.
2. In the inner pot of the pressure cooker, add the oil and press the "Meat/Chicken" button. Add the seasoned ribs and brown, putting a nice sear on all sides.
3. Mix together the remaining ingredients and stir to combine. Add the pork and coat evenly with the barbecue sauce.
4. Close the lid completely and slide the pressure valve to locked position.
5. Press the "Meat/Chicken" button and use the "Time Adjustment" feature to set the pressure cooking time to 22 minutes.
6. When the pressure cooking cycle is completed, allow the pressure to release naturally. Slide the pressure valve to open position to fully release the pressure. Open the lid when pressure has released.
7. Transfer the pork ribs to a serving platter and serve immediately with the barbecue sauce poured over the top.

PORK CARNITAS

Pork carnitas on the stove can take hours to get the pork nice and tender and then add that crunchy, yummy glaze. With the Power Pressure Cooker XL, you can get pork carnitas in under 2 hours, with very little time that requires your attention. Serve it up any way you like. Some like it in burritos, while others prefer it over a salad or rice. With this easy meal, you can't go wrong!

Ingredients:

- 2 pounds pork shoulder, boneless and cut into 2 inch chunks
- 1 tablespoon taco seasoning
- juice of 2 oranges
- juice of 1 lime
- 1 tablespoon olive oil
- salt and pepper, to taste

Preparation time: 10 minutes
cooking time:
1 hour, 40 minutes
Serves: 4 to 6

Directions:

1. Season the pork with the taco seasoning and salt and pepper.
2. Juice the oranges and lime into a measuring cup and stop off with enough water to reach the 1 cup mark. Pour the liquid into the inner pot. Add the pork.
3. Close the lid completely and slide the pressure valve to locked position.
4. Press the "Meat/Chicken" button and use the "Time Adjustment" feature to set the pressure cooking time to 50 minutes.
5. When the pressure cooking cycle is completed, press the "Keep Warm/Cancel" button and allow pressure to release naturally. Open the lid when pressure has released.
6. Press the "Meat/Chicken" button. Use a fork to shred the meat inside the pot. Bring to a boil and allow to bubble until almost all of the liquid is gone. This may take 20-30 minutes. When most of the liquid is gone, stir in the olive oil. Continue to cook for about 5 minutes until meat is beginning to brown.
7. Transfer to a serving platter or bowl and serve immediately with limes and avocado slices over a bed of rice.

BRAISED HONEY-DIJON PORK BELLY

Pork belly shouldn't just be one of those foods you only order in fancy restaurants! The Power Pressure Cooker XL takes out the guess work out of cooking this cut of meat. I guarantee, your family will request this one again!

Ingredients:

- 2 pounds of pork belly, cut into several pieces
- 6 tablespoons Dijon mustard
- ½ cup honey
- ½ cup chicken or vegetable broth
- 2 large white onions, quartered
- ¼ teaspoon chopped thyme
- Salt and black pepper, to taste
- 2 tablespoons of olive oil

Preparation time: 15 minutes
Cooking time: 45 minutes
Serves: 4 to 6

Directions:

1. In the inner pot of the pressure cooker, add the oil and press the "Meat/Chicken" button. Add pork, season to taste with salt and pepper and cook until browned evenly. Remove from the pot.
2. Stir in the onions and cook until just soft and translucent. Add in the rest of the ingredients (including the pork) and stir to combine. Press the "Keep Warm/Cancel" button.
3. Close the lid completely and slide the pressure valve to locked position.
4. Press the "Beans/Lentils" button and press the "Cook Time Selector" button twice to use the pre-programmed time of 30 minutes.
5. When the pressure cooking cycle is completed, slide the pressure valve to open position to fully release the pressure. Open the lid when pressure has released.
6. Adjust seasonings if desired, transfer into a serving bowl or platter and serve immediately.

BARBECUE PULLED PORK

This recipe is a staple at our house, especially in the summer when we love to keep some in the fridge for bbq sandwiches on busy days. The pork will take about 2 hours cook, but most of that is hands-off. The sauce it cooks it is super yummy, but feel free to add more sauce if you desire.

Ingredients:

- 2 ½ pound boneless pork shoulder
- 1 ½ cups barbecue sauce of your choice
- 1 tablespoon garlic, minced
- ¼ cup brown sugar
- 2 tablespoons Worcestershire sauce
- ¾ cup chicken or vegetable broth
- 2 tablespoons of olive oil
- Salt and black pepper, to taste

Preparation time: *15 minutes*
Cooking time: *2 hours*
Serves: *6-8*

Directions:

1. Cut the pork into two pieces and season with salt, pepper or seasonings of your choice.
2. In the inner pot of the pressure cooker, add the oil and press the "Meat/Chicken" button. Add pork to the pot and sear on all sides. Stir in the garlic and cook for another 1-2 minutes.
3. Add in the rest of the ingredients, season to taste and stir to combine. Press the "Keep Warm/Cancel" button.
4. Close the lid completely and slide the pressure valve to locked position.
5. Press the "Canning/Preserving" button and set the pressure cooking time to 90 minutes.
6. When the pressure cooking cycle is completed, allow pressure to release naturally or 10 minutes, then slide the pressure valve to open position to fully release the pressure. Open the lid when pressure has released.
7. Use a fork to shred the meat. Gently stir to coat the meat with the sauce.
8. Adjust seasonings if desired, transfer into a serving bowl and serve immediately.

PORK SAUSAGE IN ONION GRAVY

I am crazy about onions cooked in a savory gravy. And served with pork sausage it just gets even better. Feel free to substitute homemade gravy if you happen to have some around.

Ingredients:

- 1 ½ cups of canned brown gravy
- 8 medium links of pork sausage
- 1 cup beef broth
- 1 onion, sliced into rounds
- 1 teaspoon mixed Italian herbs
- 2 teaspoons of Worcestershire sauce
- Salt and pepper, to taste

Preparation time: 15 minutes
Cooking time: 40 minutes
Serves: 4 to 6

Directions:

1. In the inner pot of the pressure cooker, add 1 tablespoon of oil and press the "Meat/ Chicken" button. Add the sausage and cook until lightly browned on all sides. Removes sausage and add onions. Brown onions in oil and sausage drippings until soft and sightly browned.
2. Discard excess oil and stir in the rest of the ingredients, including the sausage. Press the "Keep Warm/Cancel" button.
3. Close the lid completely and slide the pressure valve to locked position.
4. Press the "Rice/Risotto" button, then push the "Cook Time Selector" button twice to set the pressure cooking time to 25 minutes.
5. When the pressure cooking cycle is completed, slide the pressure valve to open position to fully release the pressure. Open the lid when pressure has released.
6. Adjust seasonings if desired, transfer to a serving bowl or platter and serve immediately.

PORK CHOPS WITH DIJON SAUCE

This meal will make you guests or family think that you slaved away over dinner, but these chops couldn't be simpler to make. The Power Pressure Cooker XL insures that the pork is super tender and the creamy sauce tastes delicious. If you have any leftover sauce, try serving it over a green vegetable such as broccoli or spinach.

Ingredients:

- 4 boneless pork chops, 1 inch thick
- ¼ cup shallots or finely diced onion
- 1 cup white wine
- ¾ cup chicken broth
- ½ cup heavy cream
- 2 tablespoons Dijon mustard
- salt and pepper, to taste
- 1-2 tablespoons oil

Preparation time: *10 minutes*
Cooking time: *35 minutes*
Serves: *4*

Directions:

1. In the inner pot of the pressure cooker, add the oil and press the "Meat/Chicken" button. Add the pork and sear on both sides. Remove pork from the pot before adding the shallots. Cook until soft and fragrant, then add half the wine to deglaze the pan. Boil and scrape at any remaining browned bits. Press the "Keep Warm/Cancel" button.
2. Add the chicken broth and the pork to the pot.
3. Close the lid completely and slide the pressure valve to locked position.
4. Press the "Soup/Stew" button use the pre-programmed pressure cooking time of 10 minutes.
5. When the pressure cooking cycle is completed, allow the pressure to release naturally for 5 minutes, then slide the pressure valve to open position to fully release the pressure. Open the lid when pressure has released.
6. Remove the pork chops, cover with foil and set aside. Press the "Meat/Chicken" button on the Power Pressure Cooker XL and add the remaining wine to the pot. Bring to a boil and boil for about 3 minutes, reducing the liquid.
7. Whisk the cream and mustard into the pot, boiling for about 3 more minutes or until sauce reaches desired consistency.
8. Adjust seasonings on the pork and serve with the chops covered in the warm Dijon sauce.

PORK CHOPS AND APPLESAUCE

Ain't that swell! This is an easy dinner to pull together on a weeknight. The apples are sweetened by the brown sugar and work as a delicious topping to the pork. The boneless pork chops will be very tender. Feel free to use bone-in chops, too, just adjust your time according to their size.

Ingredients:

- 1 ½ pounds boneless pork chops
- 6 cups apples, sliced
- ½ cup brown sugar
- 2 tablespoons flour
- 1 teaspoon cinnamon
- ½ cup water
- drizzle olive oil
- Salt and black pepper, to taste

Preparation time: *10 minutes*
Cooking time: *25 minutes*
Serves: *4 to 6*

Directions:

1. In the inner pot of the pressure cooker, press the "Meat/Chicken" button and add the oil. Season the pork chops with salt and pepper, then place in the pot. Brown on both sides, then remove from the pot. Press the "Keep Warm/Cancel" button
2. In a separate bowl, toss together the apples, flour, brown sugar and cinnamon. Add the water to the inner pot and scrape at any browned bits left from the pork. Pour the apples into the pot and place the pork on top.
3. Close the lid completely and slide the pressure valve to locked position.
4. Press the "Soup/Stew" button which will automatically set the pressure cooking time to 10 minutes.
5. When the pressure cooking cycle is completed, allow the pressure to release for 5-10 minutes. Then slide the pressure valve to open position to fully release the pressure. Open the lid when pressure has released.
6. Transfer the pork chops to a plate and serve covered in the apple mixture.

MUSTARD BARBECUE SPARERIBS

Southerners take their barbecue very seriously. The mustard barbecue sauce originated in South Carolina, thought to have been developed by German settlers. Obviously it is much more "mustardy" in its flavor than its tomato- based counterparts, but not in an off-putting way. I don't like mustard on my sandwiches or hot dogs, but I love some mustard flavor in my barbecue and baked beans!

Ingredients:

- 2 pounds of pork spareribs, cut into large chunks
- 1 tablespoon of BBQ dry rub seasoning
- 1 ½ cups mustard barbecue sauce
- ½ water
- 2 tablespoons maple syrup
- 2 tablespoons of olive oil
- 2 tablespoons apple cider or balsamic vinegar
- Salt and crushed black pepper, to taste

Preparation time: 10 minutes
cooking time: 40 minutes
Serves: 4 to 6

Directions:

1. Season the pork ribs with dry rub, salt and pepper and rub it evenly on all sides. Set aside.
2. In the inner pot of the pressure cooker, add the oil and press the "Meat/Chicken" button. Add the ribs and brown evenly on both sides. Mix in the rest of the ingredients, stir to combine and press the "Keep Warm/Cancel" button.
3. Close the lid completely and slide the pressure valve to locked position.
4. Press the "Rice/Risotto" button, then push the "Cook Time Selector" button twice to set the pressure cooking time to 25 minutes.
5. When the pressure cooking cycle is completed, slide the pressure valve to open position to fully release the pressure. Open the lid when pressure has released.
6. Toss to evenly coat the ribs with the BBQ sauce, transfer to a serving platter and serve immediately with the remaining sauce on the side. To thicken the sauce, press the "Meat/Chicken" button and simmer until desired thickness is reached.

HAWAIIAN PORK ROAST

This is an easy, easy way to make a lot of food in very little time. I like to serve the shredded meat as sliders on Hawaiian sweet rolls with a small slice of pineapple or avocado . Pour the extra sauce over the top of the meat or place it in a bowl on the side for dipping.

Ingredients:

- 3 to 4 pounds of pork butt roast, sliced into several chunks
- 2 tablespoons of bacon fat
- Hawaiian sea salt and black pepper, to taste
- 1 ½ tablespoons garlic, minced
- ¼ cup onion, finely diced
- 1 cup of pineapple juice
- 2 tablespoons of brown sugar

Preparation time: 10 minutes
Cooking time:
1 hour 30 minutes
Serves: 8

Directions:

1. Season the pork with salt and black pepper and rub evenly on all areas. Set aside.
2. In the inner pot of the pressure cooker, add the bacon fat and press the "Meat/Chicken" button. Add the pork and brown evenly on all sides.Remove the pork and add the garlic and onions. Cook until soft and fragrant.
3. Return the pork back to the pot. Add in the rest of the ingredients, stir to combine and press the "Keep Warm/Cancel" button.
4. Close the lid completely and slide the pressure valve to locked position.
5. Press the "Meat/Chicken" button and press the "Cook Time Selector" key two times to set the pressure cooking time to 60 minutes.
6. When the pressure cooking cycle is completed, allow pressure to release naturally for at least 10 minutes. Slide the pressure valve to open position to fully release the pressure. Open the lid when pressure has released.
7. Transfer to a serving platter, shred or slice the meat and serve immediately with sauce on top.

SMOKY BARBECUE BABY BACK RIBS

Everyone loves Baby Back Ribs! And I love how easy they are in the Power Pressure Cooker XL. Sometimes its just too hot to grill and I don't want to wait on oven baked ribs. Use your favorite dry rub mix with spices such as paprika, garlic powder, salt, black pepper, chili powder and onion powder.

Ingredients:

- 1 ½ cups Mesquite barbecue sauce
- 3 tablespoons of BBQ dry rub seasoning
- 2 tablespoons of olive oil
- 2 pounds of baby back pork ribs, cut into 4 portions
- 2 tablespoons of apple cider or balsamic vinegar
- 2 tablespoons brown sugar
- 2 tablespoons liquid smoke
- ½ cup water

Preparation time: 10 minutes
Cooking time: 1 hour
Serves: 4 to 6

Directions:

1. Season the pork with BBQ seasoning and rub evenly on all areas. Set aside.
2. In the inner pot of the pressure cooker, add the oil and press the "Meat/Chicken" button. Add the pork and cook until evenly browned on both sides. Stir in the rest of the ingredients and mix to combine. Press the "Keep Warm/Cancel" button.
3. Close the lid completely and slide the pressure valve to locked position.
4. Press the "Meat/Chicken" button and use the "Time Adjustment" button to set the pressure cooking time to 22 minutes.
5. When the pressure cooking cycle is completed, slide the steam release handle to the venting position to fully release the pressure. Open the lid when pressure has released. Gently toss to evenly coat the ribs with the sauce.
6. Transfer the ribs to a serving platter, pour the sauce over the ribs and serve immediately.

PORK CHOPS WITH RANCH GRAVY

Kid pleasing recipe here! This recipe really couldn't be any simpler and it makes for a great, filling meal when you are in a hurry. I like to serve it with a green vegetable and some applesauce. If you don't like to use canned cream soups or pre-packaged mixes feel free to use your homemade versions.

Ingredients:

- 2 pounds of pork chops
- 1 ½ cups canned cream of chicken soup
- ¾ cup chicken broth
- Salt and pepper, to taste
- 1 packet of ranch dressing mix
- 2 tablespoons butter

Preparation time: 10 minutes
Cooking time: 30 minutes
Serves: 4 to 6

Directions:

1. Season the pork chops with salt and pepper and rub evenly on both sides. Set aside.
2. In the inner pot of the pressure cooker, add the 2 tablespoons of butter and press the "Meat/Chicken" button. Add the pork and cook until evenly browned on all sides. Add in cream of chicken soup and ½ cup broth, stir to combine and press the "Keep Warm/ Cancel" button.
3. Close the lid completely and slide the pressure valve to locked position.
4. Press the "Meat/Chicken" button which will automatically set the pressure cooking time to 15 minutes. Thicker chops will require a little longer.
5. While cooking the pork, combine together the ranch dressing and the remaining broth. Set aside.
6. When the pressure cooking cycle is completed, slide the pressure valve to open position to fully release the pressure. Open the lid when pressure has released. Stir in the ranch dressing mixture and cook further using the "Meat/Chicken" button until it reaches a boil.
7. Adjust seasonings if desired. Transfer to a serving bowl or platter and serve immediately.

Desserts

TAPIOCA PUDDING

Usually making tapioca requires the cook to have constant attention on the stove, stirring frequently and making sure the mixture doesn't boil. With the Power Pressure Cooker XL, you can literally "set it and forget it." I like to serve the pudding cold with fruit and cream, but you could also serve it warm right after cooking. Be sure to place a layer of plastic wrap over the top of the pudding to prevent a skin forming on top when you put it in the refrigerator.

Ingredients:

- ½ cup tapioca pearls, rinsed and drained
- 1 ½ cups of milk
- ¾ cup of water
- ½ cup of granulated sugar
- 1 teaspoon of lemon zest
- Whipped cream or fresh fruits, for serving (optional)

Preparation time: **10 minutes**
Cooking time: **45 minutes**
Serves: **6 to 8**

Directions:

1. Combine together all ingredients in a heat-proof bowl that fits in the inner pot of the pressure cooker. Mix it thoroughly until the sugar is dissolved completely and set aside. Prepare a foil sling by folding a piece of 18-inch aluminum foil twice, lengthwise. This is used to easily remove the baking dish from the pressure cooker after pressure cooking.

2. Pour 2 cups of water in the inner pot of the pressure cooker and place in the steamer tray. Place the bowl on the center of the foil sling and carefully place it on the prepared steamer tray inside the pressure cooker.

3. Close the lid completely and slide the pressure valve to locked position.

4. Press the "Soup/Stew" button and use the pre-programed cooking time of 10 minutes.

5. When the pressure cooking cycle is completed, turn off the pressure cooker and let it stand for about 15 to 20 minutes more before opening the lid. This allows the dessert to still cook in the pot while the pressure releases and prevents any messy spills.

6. Remove the lid carefully, when float valve drops. Use the sling to lift the bowl out of the pot and place on a hot pad or towel.

7. Stir thoroughly and portion into individual serving bowls, cover with plastic wrap and let it cool completely. Chill for at least 3 hours before serving with whipped cream or sliced fresh fruits on top.

SPICED STEWED PEARS

This is a very simple dessert that looks rather impressive. My kids were astounded at the red pears! I've found that if you slice about half an inch off the bottom of each pear it will make it easier for the pears to stand up. Want to take the taste to the next level? Two words: Ice. Cream. Vanilla ice cream goes perfect with this dessert and you will want to use any leftover syrup as a topping.

Ingredients:

- 6 medium firm pears, peeled with stem attached
- 2 ½ cups of dry red wine
- 2 teaspoons of pumpkin pie spice
- ½ cup of granulated sugar
- 1 teaspoon of orange zest
- 1 orange, juiced

Preparation time: 15 minutes
Cooking time: 25 minutes
Serves: 6

Directions:

1. In the inner pot of the pressure cooker, mix together all ingredients except for the pears and stir until the sugar is dissolved completely. Add the pears and evenly coat with the wine mixture.
2. Close the lid completely and slide the pressure valve to locked position.
3. Press the "Soup/Stew" button and use the pre-programed cooking time of 10 minutes.
4. When the pressure cooking cycle is completed, slide the steam release handle to the venting position to fully release the pressure. Open the lid when pressure has released. Carefully remove the pears using two spoons and portion into individual serving bowls.
5. Pour the sauce on top and serve.

STEWED MIXED FRUITS

Served with a large dollop of whipped cream, this is a yummy dessert that seems particularly pleasing in the fall. Cooking the dried fruits in the pressure cooker plumps them up and makes them juicy, yet still chewier than a traditional mixed fruit. Try any of your favorite dried fruits. Some of my favorites are prunes, apples, cherries and apricots.

Ingredients:

- 1 cup of apple juice
- ¼ cup dry red wine
- ¾ cup of brown sugar
- 1 teaspoon of ground cinnamon
- 1 lemon, sliced into wedges
- 1 pound of mixed dried fruits

Preparation time: 5 minutes
Cooking time: 45 minutes
Serves: 6

Directions:

1. In the inner pot of the pressure cooker, mix together the juice, wine, sugar and cinnamon and stir until the sugar is dissolved completely. Add in the lemon and mixed dried fruits and toss to evenly coat the fruits with the dissolved sugar mixture.
2. Close the lid completely and slide the pressure valve to locked position.
3. Press the "Soup/Stew" button and use the pre-programed cooking time of 10 minutes.
4. When the pressure cooking cycle is completed, let the pressure release naturally until pressure has released. Let it stand for about 10 to 15 minutes before opening the lid and let it cool completely.
5. Gently stir to coat the fruits with the sauce, portion into individual serving bowls and serve topped with whipped cream if desired.

CRANBERRY-APPLE SAUCE

We are applesauce crazy in our house. For some reason, perhaps its the addition of the cranberries, but this applesauce has become a staple in our house for Thanksgiving leftovers. As in, you can't eat a turkey sandwich without a side of this applesauce. The cranberries add a nice tangy flavor that really compliments the apples. And the Power Pressure Cooker XL makes it super easy to prepare.

Ingredients:

- 4-5 large apples, core-removed and diced
- 1 ½ cups cranberry juice
- ½ cup dried cranberries
- 1 cup brown sugar
- 2 tablespoons of lemon juice
- 1 teaspoon of cinnamon

Preparation time: 15 minutes
Cooking time: 35 minutes
Serves: 4

Directions:

1. In the inner pot of the pressure cooker, mix together all ingredients and stir until the sugar is fully dissolved.
2. Close the lid completely and slide the pressure valve to locked position.
3. Press the "Rice/Risotto" button and use "Time Adjustment" feature to set the pressure cooking time to 8 minutes.
4. When the pressure cooking cycle is completed, allow the pressure to release naturally. Open the lid when pressure has released. Stir the mixture.
5. Let it cool completely. Serve it as a chunky compote or transfer the mixture into a food processor and process until smooth. Store in sealed jars or containers and chill before serving.

MINI MOLTEN CHOCOLATE CAKES

Nothing is tastier and more simple than these molten cakes. This would make the perfect dessert for a special occasion, but is easy enough to do any night of the week. This one is sure to satisfy all of your chocolate cravings!

Ingredients:

- 1 egg
- 4 tablespoons sugar
- 4 tablespoons milk
- 4 tablespoons all purpose flour
- 1 tablespoon cocoa powder
- ½ teaspoon baking powder
- 2 tablespoons olive oil
- pinch of salt

Preparation time: 5 minutes
Cooking time: 20 minutes
Serves: 3

Directions:

1. Lightly spray three 4-ounce ramekins with cooking spray.
2. In a mixing bowl, stir together all of the ingredients until well incorporated. Pour them into the ramekins, dividing the mixture evenly.
3. Pour 1 cup of water into the inner pot of the pressure cooker. Add a steamer tray and place the prepared ramekins on the steamer tray.
4. Close the lid completely and slide the pressure valve to locked position.
5. Press the "Rice/Risotto" button and use the pre-programmed time of 6 minutes. This will produce the molten effect with the gooey chocolate. If you prefer your cake more set, set the timer for 9 minutes.
6. When the pressure cooking cycle is completed, perform a quick release of the pressure. Remove the lid when the float valve has dropped.
7. Carefully remove the ramekins from the inner pot. Dust with powdered sugar if desired and serve warm.

THREE LAYER MAGIC CAKE

The Magic cake is a three layer cake all baked with one batter in one pan. The first layer is a fudge layer, followed by custard and topped with sponge cake. The batter can be a little tricky to get right, so take the time to really beat the egg whites until stiff. And mix all the ingredients until they are silky and smooth.

Ingredients:

- 4 eggs
- 3/4 cup sugar
- 3/4 cup flour
- 1 tablespoon vanilla extract
- 1 stick butter, melted
- 2 cups of milk, heated to warm

Preparation time: *10 minutes*
Cooking time: *1 hour*
Serves: *6*

Directions:

1. In the inner pot of the pressure cooker, add 2 cups water and place your steamer tray. Prepare your 7-inch springform pan.

2. Separate the yolks from the whites of the eggs. Beat the whites until they begin to form stiff peaks. In another bowl, blend the yolks and the sugar until well mixed.

3. Add the melted butter and vanilla to the egg yolks. Continue to blend with a mixer. Add the flour slowly until all is well incorporated. Pour in the warm milk, a little at a time and mix well.

4. Spoon in the egg whites, a large spoonful at a time until all have been added. Make sure batter is well combined and pour into the springform pan.

5. Create a sling by folding and 18-inch piece of aluminum foil in half twice lengthwise. Use this to help get the springform pan in and out of the inner pot. Place springform pan on the sling and lower onto the steamer tray. Cover the pan loosely with foil.

6. Close the lid completely and slide the pressure valve to locked position.

7. Press the "Meat/Chicken" button and push "Cook Time Selector" button to set the pressure cooking time to 40 minutes.

8. When the pressure cooking cycle is completed, slide the steam release handle to the venting position to fully release the pressure. Open the lid when pressure has released. Carefully use the sling to remove the pan and set aside to allow to cool.

9. Dust with powdered sugar and serve when cool.

Made in the USA
Lexington, KY
30 December 2017